# Praise for Secret Stuff

Almost two thousand years ago Jesus was examined by Pilate before His crucifixion and subsequent resurrection. Jesus told Pilate that he was testifying of the truth and everyone who hears His voice follows the truth. Pilate responded mockingly by asking, "What is truth?" Today this seems to be the anguished cry of our age. Landon Scholl is a serious student of the truth and wants people to not only know the truth but to follow the truth — Jesus Christ! This book will help students find the truth in Jesus.

—Dr. Rod Dempsey
Director of the Master of Arts in Christian Ministry
Liberty University School of Divinity

Landon loves the Lord and the Word. In *Secret Stuff*, he calls the next generation to a God-centered view of the world. His passion to see young people uncover real hope is evident as he tackles relevant issues like truth, morality, and the inerrancy of Scripture. This work engages both steadfast followers of Jesus and seekers, and is certain to provoke rich conversation of important topics.

—Dr. Bill Curtis
Senior Pastor, Cornerstone Baptist Church, Darlington, SC
Award-Winning Author, *Engaging Exposition*,
*30 Days to James*, and *Exalting Jesus in Micah*

As a believer, my later High School and early college years were the most spiritually challenging and trying times in my life. I often felt adrift at sea, constantly attacked by the sharks of scientific naturalism, situational ethics, and sexual immorality. I wish I would have had a resource like Secret Stuff and someone like Landon to help navigate me and anchor my life upon truth. This book is a rare combination of apologetics and Christ-centered biblical theology. It will be a useful tool for those wanting to make disciples and strengthen the faith of young believers. I am glad to have such a resource for the students in my ministry that will encourage them to defend their faith and grow in the grace and knowledge of our Lord and Savior Jesus Christ.

—Dr. Dwayne Milioni
Lead Pastor, Open Door Church Raleigh NC
Assistant Professor of Preaching, Southeastern
Baptist Theological Seminary
Board Chairman, The Pillar Church Planting Network

*Fear not for I am with you;*
*do not be afraid for I am your God;*
*I will strengthen you, I will help you,*
*I will uphold you with my righteous right hand.*
**ISAIAH 41:10**

# SECRET STUFF

## LANDON SCHOLL

Seed Publishing Group, LLC
Timmonsville, South Carolina

*Secret Stuff*

Published by:
Seed Publishing Group
2570 Double C Farm Ln
Timmonsville, SC 29161
seed–publishing–group.com

Edited by:
Cassie Martin

Cover Art by:
Dustin Phelps

Illustrations by:
Kerri Smith

Seed Publishing Group is committed to bringing great resources to both individual Christians and the local church (please visit them at www.seed-publishing-group.com). As part of that commitment, they are partners with The Pillar Network for church planting (www.thepillarnetwork.com). $1 from each sale of *Secret Stuff* goes directly to church plants throughout North America. Thank you for purchasing *Secret Stuff*, and thank you for investing in church planting!

To order additional copies of this resource visit
www.seed–publishing–group.com.

Library of Congress Control Number: 2018940457
ISBN–13: 978-0-9985451-3-4

*Printed in the United States of America*

*To my parents, for your love, for your support, for your faith.*

# CONTENTS

# INTRODUCTION

'The Roaring Twenties' recalls images of flappers, jazz music, and F. Scott Fitzgerald. It was a peaceful and prosperous time after World War I and before the Great Depression. Prohibition was a key political movement that pushed alcohol underground and inadvertently founded the speakeasy business — another icon of the Jazz Age. History reveals that, despite prosperity and the excitement of new media and culture, a generation of hope-seekers grew disillusioned and depressed.

Like the lost generation of the 1920s, we live in a time of relative prosperity and peace. We have access to every pleasure and comfort, yet stress, anxiety, and depression persist. Our generation struggles to find meaning and joy because culture has told us that there is no truth, no answer to life's questions, and no eternity. We are living in a new Prohibition — hope has been pushed underground.

Secret Stuff invites readers to knock on the sacred door of eternal truth, where hope and peace can be found. This book explores biblical foundations for Truth, Origin, Identity, Meaning, Morality, and Destiny. Topics can be read individually or collectively, as each unveil the only source of lasting joy: the reality and grace of Jesus Christ.

—Cassie Martin

# TRUTH

*And you will know the truth, and the truth will set you free.*
**JOHN 8:32**

*If you look for truth, you may find comfort in the end; if you look for comfort you will not get neither comfort nor truth, only soft soap and wishful thinking to begin, and in the end, despair.*
**C.S. LEWIS**

*Every word of God proves true; He is a shield to those who take refuge in Him.*
**AGUR SON OF JAKEH**

*Truth is so obscure in these times, and falsehood so established, that, unless we love the truth, we cannot know it.*
**BLAISE PASCAL**

*Sanctify them in truth; your word is truth.*
**JESUS**

*There is no middle ground. What is not true is false.*
**HENRY F. KLETZING**

*The man who lies to himself and listens to his own lie comes to a point that he cannot distinguish the truth within him, or around him, and so loses all respect for himself and for others.*
**FYODOR DOSTOEVSKY**

# TRUTH

## RIGHT IN FRONT OF US

Truth is a Big Deal! What you believe about truth has enormous consequence. Life or death consequence. Think for a moment about the *truth* of crossing the street. Say you begin to cross the street with a good friend. Of course you stop, look, and listen just like Mrs. Smith taught you in grade school and then proceed to cross. Before you take a second step your friend grabs your arm, yanks you backward, and a screaming Mack truck barrels past your nose at 55 mph. Whew!

No one in their right mind is going to turn around, look their friend square in the eye and scream, "What do you think you are doing?!" "I don't know," your friend will reply, "Saving your life?!" That's a five-star friend. Why? Because the truth of the matter is that they did save your life. Why have they saved your life? Because a Mack truck traveling at a speed of 55 mph + a human being crossing in front of it = a dead human being.

But you will say to your friend, "I don't believe Mack trucks can hurt me." To which your friend will respond in kind, "I love you, but you are crazy." "I believe truth is whatever I believe it to be," you say, "and I believe Mack trucks cannot hurt me." "Okay." Your friend replies, "Here comes another one."

So that is a little far-fetched, but not really. I mean you have most likely learned that when it comes to laws of physics and mathematics there is truth and error. Your test scores have proven this true. You have most likely also learned that when it comes to matters of religion or morality or sexuality there is only opinion. Truth, if ever has accompanied these realms, you hear, 'has since deserted at the presence of advanced human reason.' "Truth, in matters of religion," as Oscar Wilde said, "is simply the *opinion* that has survived."[1] Was Wilde right? Are matters of religion only opinion? For that matter, are matters of morality subjective? Is truth whatever we want it to be?

Like any good theory, it must be tested. Test the theory that the gorgeous guy or girl liked you in high school. The theory that she was into you was proven false when she laughed in your face and stormed down the hall after you asked her out. Let's test the theory that morality is subjective. Said another way, is the idea that what is right for you isn't right for me, true? Can morality be whatever we want it to be?

## RIGHT AND WRONG

C.S. Lewis has really done most of the leg work in this area. His argument is pretty simple and mostly follows like this:

1. People will say that absolute morality is only an opinion
2. Yet people appeal to absolute morality when seeking justice

3. Therefore, people must acknowledge that morality is not mere preference, but objective reality

He says it more fully like this:

> I know that some people say the idea of a Law of Nature or decent behavior known to all men is unsound, because different civilizations and different ages have had quite different moralities.
>
> But this is not true. There have been differences between their moralities, but these have never amounted to anything like a total difference. If anyone will take the trouble to compare the moral teaching of, say, the ancient Egyptians, Babylonians, Hindus, Chinese, Greeks and Romans, what will really strike him will be how very like they are to each other and to our own. ...
>
> But the most remarkable thing is this. Whenever you find a man who says he does not believe in a real Right and Wrong, you will find the same man going back on this a moment later. He may break his promise to you, but if you try breaking one to him he will be complaining "It's not fair" before you can say Jack Robinson. A nation may say treaties do not matter, but then, next minute, they spoil their case by saying that the particular treaty they want to break was an unfair one. But if treaties do not matter, and if there is no such thing as Right and Wrong— in other words, if there is no Law

of Nature—what is the difference between a fair treaty and an unfair one? Have they not let the cat out of the bag and shown that, whatever they say, they really know the Law of Nature just like anyone else?

It seems, then, we are forced to believe in a real Right and Wrong. People may be sometimes mistaken about them, just as people sometimes get their sums wrong; but they are not a matter of mere taste and opinion any more than the multiplication table.[2]

When the theory 'morality is subjective' is tested, we find that men and women of all civilizations in all times have agreed that the 'Law of Nature,' as C.S. Lewis calls it, is objective. Morality is an entity entirely outside of human jurisdiction. Humanity lacks the authority to change or rewrite right and wrong. When, Hitler tried to strip a people group of their inherent rights, the world responded with furious condemnation. We inherently know when something violates moral law.

Be careful not to imagine that the idea of subjective morality will hold up in real life situations. If you put a murderer, a rapist, a nun, and a thief in a room and tell them that morality is whatever they want it to be, I am not confident anyone would make it out alive. We have laws against stealing, and murder, and rape because society needs these laws to function. But these laws were not written by the advancement of reason so society could move forward. These laws belong to a code of ethics written deep within human consciousness, etched as if upon eternal stone by an eternal hand. These laws were given to humans, not by humans. It is simply humanity's duty to keep and protect them, to her joy.

# TRUTH AND RELIGION

Deep in our hearts, we inherently sense the difference between right and wrong. We know truth exists. But, is there truth in religion? Is a certain religion true? Are all religions true? Before we tackle all those big questions, let me ask you one. In math class, did you keep working for the correct answer once your answer matched the one in the back of the book (BOB)? Or, when you first raced to the back of the book to fill in your homework with all of the odd answers — and then scribbled down some numbers above it to make it look like you completed the work with Einstein efficiency — did you worry about proving the answer? No. You assumed the BOB got it right. Well, if you had my luck you were the first to be called on to give the answer in class. And, of course, after you questionably stated the answer, as if to fake the struggle you bore in coming to your conclusion, in hopes the teacher will move on, she asks, "And how did you come to your answer?" *Seriously?!?! I don't know, that is just what the back of the book had lady!*

Sadly, most people live their lives based off of what other people have told them and have no idea how they arrived at that answer. You've heard 'Truth is whatever you believe it is.' *Okay, how do we know that?* 'Truth is objective,' some say. *Okay, but why?* We should want to see the proof before we stake our lives on it.

One thing we do know about truth is that it is exclusive. The law of non-contradiction does not allow a sane person to say that a bird can simultaneously be a bee. Contrary to what you may have heard this also applies to matters of religion. If one religion or belief system says that heaven is real while another says it is not real, both cannot be right. There is either a heaven or there is not. We cannot say, 'yeah Hinduism is true for you but Christianity is right for me.' The idea that opposing truth claims can be

21

true at the same time is bonkers. I can't get to heaven by pleasing Allah (Islam) and at the same time get to heaven by repenting and believing in Jesus (Christianity). They are two very different truth statements and both cannot be true. And the same can be said when comparing all world religions. Not all truth claims are true. Not all roads lead to heaven.

The nature of truth, namely its exclusivity, makes our search for truth a little easier. Once we find the truth we don't have to keep searching for the right answer. So in our search for truth among world religions I want to start with Christianity. I want to start here because every other religion claims to teach truth; *Jesus claimed that he is Truth*. And that my friends, is a very BIG difference.

## TRUTH AND THE BIBLE

If we are going to talk about Jesus, we are going to have to talk about the Bible because the majority of what we know about him is in that book. Now, the Bible is pretty impressive, but if it isn't true then what we know about Jesus most likely isn't true. However, if the Bible is true then we are really going to have to take its truth claims seriously.

I could rattle off some pretty amazing facts about the Bible. I could tell you it was Written in three languages (Hebrew, Aramaic, and Greek), on three continents (Asia, Africa, and Europe), over a span of 1500 years, by more than 40 authors, and yet retains a harmonious narrative and purpose. I could tell you that the Bible is *the most historically reliable text of antiquity*. The Dead Sea Scrolls for instance (discovered AD 1946-56, 2017) have manuscripts dated as early as the 150 BC and as late as 70 AD. These texts provide scholars with great verification about the reliability of Scripture. There are over 24,000 New Testament manuscripts, of which, more than 5,000 are complete. Some New

Testament manuscripts, such as the John Rylands Library Papyrus P52, date to c. 175 AD. Very conservatively estimated, this falls within 100 years of the completion of the New Testament. Behind the Bible, the second closest verified work of antiquity is Homer's *Illiad*. Written in 900 BC, there are only 643 surviving manuscript copies, the earliest dating to 400 BC, which leaves a 500 year gap!

I could tell you that the New Testament was written in its entirety within 70 years of Christ's death. To compare, the seven extant plays of Sophocles were written 1400 years after Sophocles penned the plays, yet the reliability of Sophocles' plays are not questioned. I could tell you that the accuracy of the New Testament is supported by extra-biblical sources. Alone, the writings of the early church fathers including Justin Martyr, Irenaeus, Clement of Alexandria, Origen, Tertullian, Hippolytus, and Eusebius could reproduce the entire New Testament. That's a lot of textual evidence, and we haven't scratched the surface.

You probably are still not impressed. 'This only tells me that the Bible I have in my hands today says what it said when it was written,' you say. 'It doesn't prove the Bible is true.' Okay, I will grant you that this amazing evidence of textual accuracy only tells me the Bible has the same words it had two thousand years ago. But are those words true?

Archaeology seems to think so. Take for example Sodom and Gomorrah. For a long time scholars did not even believe those places existed. They believed them to be myths created to teach a spiritual lesson.[3] And then archaeologists found them situated right where the Bible described their location. And guess what else they found? Evidence of destruction by an earthquake and brimstone, just as the Bible describes in Genesis 19. That's pretty good evidence right? Well, there's more.

According to British archaeologist John Garstang, Jericho is another proof of the truth of the words of the Bible. In ancient wars, armies pushed walls from the outside-in to attack a city. That makes sense because if you are on the outside you can't push from the inside. But, at the archeological dig of Jericho, Garstang found that the walls fell outward — unlike any other attacked city in history. It matched the biblical account of Joshua 6. The walls fell inside-out in a manner impossible for an attacking force to induce unless they had some supernatural help.

Then you have archeological finds like the Merneptah Stele found in 1896 in Thebes, Egypt which dates to 1209 BC and contains the first mention of Israel outside of the Old Testament. This dating matches almost exactly the time Joshua led Israel into Canaan (1400BC-1200BC). The Mesha Stele or the Moabite Stone discovered in 1868 in Dibon, Moab dates to 850 BC. The inscribed stone lists Omri, Ahab, and King Mesha evidencing the Moabites mentioned in 1 & 2 Kings were real. King Omri, the sixth king of Israel, and his son King Ahab, are all proven to be historical figures.

Interested in more? The Cyrus Cylinder, an ancient clay cylinder, was discovered in Babylon, Mesopotamia by Hormuzd Rassam in March 1879. This artifact dates to 518 BC and records the conquest of the city of Babylon in 586 BC, proving the biblical account of Daniel 5. Similarly, the Tell Dan Inscription, discovered in the 1930s in northern Israel contains the first reference outside of the OT to David. This ancient near east artifact dating to 850 BC is just another small stone in the mountain of evidence that supports the truth of the Bible.

This type of biblical vindication is legion. The archeological evidence to support the Bible could fill the pages of volumes of books. I do not want to bore you with all the artifacts, but if you want to see for yourself, resources are available for you to delve into this area of evidence even more deeply. [4] But, let's not get lost in the evidence. The overarching point is that as we discover more of history through archeology, we find that the Bible's record of history is accurate. The Bible's words prove to be true.

# PROPHECY

Perhaps one of the most remarkable aspects of the Bible is its ability to be tested. 'Prophecy' is the word used by the Bible to make a factual statement about a future event. The Bible doesn't make generic statements like it will rain next year or there will be a famine sometime. The Bible makes statements that can be proven either true or false. The Bible makes statements as specific as a man from 1893 living in the Bronx saying that in 2018 there will be a place where people will eat chicken, with waffle fries and sweet tea, and the name of that place will be Chick-fil-A, and there will be a Chick-fil-A on Jones Street in Louisville, KY and the owner's name will be Dave. A detailed statement like that is easily proven true or false in time. Either there will be this so called Chick-fil-A or not. Depending on the outcome of his word, people will ultimately call him crazy or God.

One of my favorite prophecies was made by the prophet Isaiah around 700 BC concerning a king named Cyrus. Cyrus was not a contemporary of Isaiah's. In fact Cyrus didn't even exist. Actually, Cyrus' parents most likely weren't even born yet. However in the book of Isaiah, writing 150 years before his reign, Isaiah not only knows Cyrus' name, but his future. This is what he said:

> Who (God) says of Cyrus, "He is my shepherd, and he shall fulfill all my purpose"; saying of Jerusalem, "She shall be built," and of the temple, "Your foundation shall be laid." (Isaiah 44:28)

> Thus says the Lord to his anointed, to Cyrus, whose right hand I have grasped, to subdue nations before him and to loose the belts of kings,

to open doors before him that gates may not be closed: "I will go before you and level the exalted places, I will break in pieces the doors of bronze and cut through the bars of iron, I will give you the treasures of darkness and the hoards in secret places, that you may know that it is I, the Lord, the God of Israel, who call you by your name. For the sake of my servant Jacob, and Israel my chosen, I call you by your name, I name you, though you do not know me. I am the Lord, and there is no other, besides me there is no God; I equip you, though you do not know me that people may know, from the rising of the sun and from the west, that there is none besides me; I am the Lord, and there is no other. I form light and create darkness; I make well-being and create calamity; I am the Lord, who does all these things. "Shower, O heavens, from above, and let the clouds rain down righteousness; let the earth open, that salvation and righteousness may bear fruit; let the earth cause them both to sprout; I the Lord have created it. "Woe to him who strives with him who formed him, a pot among earthen pots! Does the clay say to him who forms it, 'What are you making?' or 'Your work has no handles'? Woe to him who says to a father, 'What are you begetting? Or to a woman, 'With what are you in labor?'" Thus says the Lord, the Holy One of Israel, and the one who formed him: "Ask me of things to come; will you command me concerning my children and the work of my hands? I made the earth and created man on it; it was my hands that stretched out the heavens, and I commanded all their host.

I have stirred him up in righteousness, and I will
make all his ways level; he shall build my city and
set my exiles free, not for price or reward," says
the Lord of hosts. (Isaiah 45:1-13)

That is awesome. You know why? Because 150 years later
(539 BC) not only is there a king named Cyrus, but he does exactly what the Bible said he would do. He allowed the people of
Israel to leave the captivity they existed under in Babylon and go
to Jerusalem. Not only were they allowed to return to Jerusalem,
they were commissioned to build the temple of God which had
been destroyed by the Babylonian king Nebuchadnezzar in 586
BC. Even more remarkably, Cyrus would pay. Here was Cyrus'
decree recorded by the prophet Ezra:

In the first year of Cyrus king of Persia, that
the word of the Lord by the mouth of Jeremiah
might be fulfilled, the Lord stirred up the spirit
of Cyrus king of Persia, so that he made a proclamation throughout all his kingdom and also
put it in writing: "Thus says Cyrus king of Persia:
The Lord, the God of heaven, has given me all
the kingdoms of the earth, and he has charged
me to build him a house at Jerusalem, which is
in Judah. Whoever is among you of all his people, may his God be with him, and let him go up
to Jerusalem, which is in Judah, and rebuild the
house of the Lord, the God of Israel—he is the
God who is in Jerusalem. And let each survivor,
in whatever place he sojourns, be assisted by the
men of his place with silver and gold, with goods
and with beasts, besides freewill offerings for the
house of God that is in Jerusalem." (Ezra 1:1-4)

In 609 BC, the prophet Jeremiah said that for 70 years the people of Israel would suffer under Babylon. Babylon got crushed by Cyrus (Persia) in 539 BC, exactly 70 years after Jeremiah's prophecy. And as you already know, Cyrus let God's people return to Jerusalem that same year (539 BC). In his *Antiquities of the Jews*, historian Flavius Josephus states that Cyrus let Israel go because he was so amazed by the prophecy he had read concerning him. Josephus records Cyrus' own words:

> Thus saith Cyrus the King: since God Almighty hath appointed me to be King of the habitable earth, I believe that He is that God, which the nation of the Israelites worship. For indeed he foretold my name by the Prophets, and that I should build him an house at Jerusalem, in the country of Judea.

It is very clear that Cyrus, the most powerful man on earth at the time, knew that the words of God are true because they proved to be true. It seems from his own words that he even believed Israel's God to be the God over all. Remarkably, the proof of the truthfulness of Scripture through the fulfillment of prophecy is sprinkled all over the Scriptures.

The Wise Men, who show up bearing gifts in all the Christmas nativities you see, saw 'his' (Jesus') star, prophesied thousands of years before in Numbers 24:17. The time of Jesus' death was prophesied by the prophet Daniel (Dan. 9: 21-26) 500 years before Jesus showed up on the scene. The prophet Micah, over 700 years before Jesus was born, said he would be born in Bethlehem (Mic. 5:2). Isaiah, prophesying more than 700 years before Jesus, said that he would be born miraculously of a virgin and, accordingly, his name would be called 'God with Us' (Isaiah 7:14).

Let us pause for one moment and discuss the idea that some people have purported that the word 'virgin' here only means a young woman of marriageable age. Without getting into a word study about the Hebrew words *almah* (עַלְמָה) or *betulah* (בְּתוּלָה) I would like to make a few observations supporting the traditional idea that *virgin* means 'never had sex,' based on the following facts: 1. Mary asks the angel who tells her she is going to bear the Son of God how it is possible for her to have a child since she had never been with a man (Luke 1:34). 2. It takes an angel to convince Joseph not to divorce Mary from their betrothal (Matt. 1:19-20). Obviously Joseph, God, and angels know how babies are normally created and recognized this conception was a miracle. 3. Mary was living under the Mosaic Law, a code of ethics that confined *all* sexual relations to marriage. Mary would have put her life on the line in breaking them (Deut. 22). 4. Isaiah calls Jesus' name 'God with Us.' A man and woman can only conceive a human — not a God. 5. The Hebrew scholars, translating the Old Testament into Greek 200 years before the birth of Christ, used the specific Greek word for virgin, parthenos, (παρθένος) referring explicitly to sexual virginity, rather than the more generic word for a young woman.

Other remarkable prophecies include Daniel's prediction of the succession of the four empires Babylon, Medo-Persia, Greece and Rome as well as the rise of Alexander the Great and the division of his Macedonian empire by his four generals; (Daniel 7:6, 8:5–8, 11:2–4) Isaiah's prophecy that Babylon would be permanently overthrown; (Isaiah 13:19; 14:23) Nahum's prophecy that Nineveh would be destroyed by fire (Nahum 3:15). These remarkably accurate prophecies are only the tip of the iceberg concerning biblical prophecy. Actually, there are 1,817 prophecies of some nature in the Bible. To date, every prophecy that has reached its maturity has proven true.

# JESUS

Jesus also affirmed the inherent truthful nature of the Bible. He believed so strongly in the obvious truthful nature of the Bible that he said that if people did not believe the Bible inherently they would not believe even if a dead man would rise to tell them it is true (Luke 16:31). Jesus affirmed that the people of the Old Testament were actual people: Abraham, Isaac, Jacob, David, Solomon, The Queen of Sheba, Elijah, Elisha, Zachariah, and others. He said that the narratives of the OT, so often written off as myths by critical scholars, were factual: Circumcision, Manna, David and Bread of the Presence, David writing certain Psalms, Moses writing the Law, Suffering of the Prophets, Lot's Wife, Sodom and Gomorrah, Tyre and Sidon. He even affirmed the controversial stories of Genesis: Adam and Eve, Cain and Abel, and the Flood in Noah's day. He confirmed the account of Jonah and the great fish to be a historical episode. He affirmed the authors of disputed books, such as Daniel (Matthew 24:15) and Isaiah (Matthew 8:17) were written by the titled individual. He also affirmed that He was the fulfillment of prophecy (Luke 4:21).

We have seen that the words of the Bible prove to be true. We have more reason to believe the words of the Bible than any other work of literature. No other book of antiquity or contemporary times has proven accurate in matters of prophecy. Therefore, the Bible's account of Jesus' words can be trusted. Even without all other proofs, we have ample evidence to believe that the words of Jesus can be trusted because he himself set his words to the test. On multiple occasions he stated that he was going to be crucified and rise from the dead three days later (Luke 24:7, 26; Matt. 16:21). Such a bold and specific statement would emphatically prove to be either true or false. With overwhelming evidence, we can believe that Jesus, in fact, did rise from the dead like he said he would.

Gary Habermas, one of the world's leading scholars on the resurrection of Jesus, offers a few minimal facts, accepted by critical biblical scholars, which verify the resurrection of Christ. He offers them essentially as follows:

1. Jesus died by crucifixion at the hands of Roman soldiers.
2. Jesus was buried in a known tomb.
3. The Tomb of Jesus was found empty three days after the crucifixion of Jesus.
4. Jesus appeared bodily to hundreds of witnesses after his resurrection.
5. The disciples of Jesus were sincerely convinced that he rose from the dead and appeared to them, and died for this fact.
6. Paul (aka Saul of Tarsus), who was a persecutor of the Christians, and James (brother of Jesus), who was a skeptic of the Christian faith, suddenly changed their beliefs towards Christianity. [5]

We could spend much time examining these claims, but I will allow you to do that on your own. I am confident you will find them to be true. We have seen that the Bible proves to be true. We have seen that the words of Jesus prove to be true, including his claim to rise from the dead. If the Bible's words about Jesus can be trusted, and Jesus' words about the Bible can be trusted, it seems that we have come to a remarkable conclusion: the Bible is true.

If we have found the Bible to be true, and there is undeniable reason to believe so, then the words of Jesus are true. Here, we return to Jesus' statement that he is Truth. He actually says, 'I am the way, the truth, and the life. No one comes to the Father except through me.' Thus, if Jesus' words are true, and the Bible's words are true, then we have found the truth – the Bible as the revealed truth concerning God's written words, and Jesus as Truth inherently. If Jesus himself is the truth, by definition there can be no other. His own claims eliminate the truth claims of every other religion. If other religions hold elements of the truth, it is only because they borrowed them from the Truth.

Though we have been taught to scoff at the notion of absolute truth, perhaps it is more appropriate to rejoice. Like a man who has searched for his true love rejoices in finding her, so human souls might rejoice at discovering the truth. After all failed attempts to fly, it is a joy to soar in pleasures of flight. Perhaps we might soar in pleasures of truth because answers about where we are from, who we are, where we might find meaning, what is right, what is wrong, and what is to come have been right in front of us all along. Maybe the truth has been set before us with tender grace to guide us into joy and confidence in the midst of a sea of uncertainty. Maybe every existential question you have had clawing at your soul like an unquenchable hunger pang can be satisfied. Could it be that all of the false assertions of truth which have left you fumbling for hope can be replaced by a foundation that is ageless and sure? 'Fairer than all fancies is the truth,' Caroline Spencer eloquently wrote. Maybe the fantasies that have left us unhappy can be replaced by the fantastic understanding that truth is right here in front of us. And, even more fantastic — that Truth loves us and seeks our joy.

# ORIGIN

*Who is like you, O LORD, among the gods? Who is like you, majestic in holiness, awesome in glorious deeds, doing wonders?*

**MOSES**


*As well might a gnat seek to drink in the ocean, as a finite creature to comprehend the Eternal God. A God whom we could understand would be no God. If we could grasp Him, He could not be infinite. If we could understand Him, He could not be divine.*

**CHARLES SPURGEON**


*Our God is in the heavens; He does whatever He pleases.*

**PSALM 115:3**


*I find it as difficult to understand a scientist who does not acknowledge the presence of a superior rationality behind the existence of the universe as it is to comprehend a theologian who would deny the advances of science.*

**WERNHER VON BRAUN**


*All the people of the earth are nothing compared to him. He does as he pleases among the angels of heaven and among the people of the earth.*

**NEBUCHADNEZZAR, KING OF BABYLON**


*Amazing fine tuning occurs in the laws that make this [complexity] possible. Realization of the complexity of what is accomplished makes it very difficult not to use the word 'miraculous' without taking a stand as to the ontological status of the word.*

**GEORGE ELLIS**

# ORIGIN
## THE POWER OF THE WORD

## COOKIES

I would like to introduce you to an idea. I'm not telling you to make her your own, but I'm asking you to give her a chance. She's not very outgoing, but she is lovely. She's not loud, but she is true. She is ancient, but vibrant. Here she is: Everything material was created. All things were spoken into existence by a Word — a glory of unapproachable light and a power of unfathomable magnitude. The idea is beautiful. There was *no* material thing and then there was *every*thing; there was darkness and then there was light. It is an idea that resonates with the human soul but, of late, has been ushered from its seat at the table of the modern mind.

Since the enlightenment, the idea of 'scientific proof' has made the idea of faith in something or someone beyond the observable seem far-fetched. But is it silly to believe that all that you see had a creator? No human had a lawn chair and a koozie to sit back and observe the beginning of the universe, so how can you prove it? The logic of deduction must be applied to the situation to arrive at a viable conclusion. Jurors all over the world use this form of logic every day to determine guilt or innocence, and in some instances, whether people will live or die.

Take for instance the Samoa Girl Scout cookies that you bought and placed in your bedroom before going to practice. When you returned home, you found that your twin sister, who was angry with you for stealing her boyfriend, was home alone with an empty box of Samoa cookies beside her. She was in a state of emotional turmoil displayed by her pithy attitude towards you and the fact that she had not showered or changed out of her pajamas in three days. Oh, and did I mention that there were Samoa remnants smothered all over her face and hands and she showed symptoms of a sugar rush? Can we prove that your sister ate the cookies? Well, not observably. We would need video evidence to prove 'scientifically' that your lovely sister devoured your cookies. We could even pump her stomach along with all those cookies and still not 'prove' they were *your* cookies. But the jury doesn't need to see video evidence to convict.

Rest assured the jury of Mom and Dad would convict even after hearing your sister's defense. They would convict based on the evidence because your sister is guilty *beyond a reasonable doubt.* Said another way, there is no other logical explanation which can be derived from the facts except that your sister committed the crime, thereby overcoming the presumption that she is innocent until proven guilty. Let the court rule that she must make restitution to you in the form of two, no three, boxes of Samoa Girl Scout cookies. Sweet justice.

No one is really going to question our sample conviction. But, when the same rules of deductive logic are applied to the verdict that *'beyond a reasonable doubt'* the universe was created, the mob cries that the evidence is not sufficient: "Unless you can show us the verifiable, tangible evidence then the ruling is invalid!"

Do we need observed evidence in every instance? I do not believe we want the burden of 'proof' applied to our neighbor whom we found in our home, holding a smoking gun, standing over the body of our lover, whom no one saw pull the trigger. In that instance everyone is crying for justice and *'beyond a reasonable doubt'* will more than suffice. Should the jury return from deliberation after two minutes and say, "We can't convict because there were no witnesses," everyone is going to shout, "What do you mean you can't convict because no one saw the murder?! That neighbor is guilty; there is no other logical explanation based on the presented evidence!"

Juries begin with evidence to reach a verdict. When one takes a look at the evidence of a created or non-created universe, it seems that we are able to reach a decision *'beyond a reasonable doubt.'* Were you to present the case for the creation of the universe before a jury, it would be hard to believe that they would, in good faith, return a verdict of 'Not Created.'

# THE GLORY OF CREATION

When observing the glory of creation, King David states:

The heavens declare the glory of God, and the sky above proclaims his handiwork. Day to day pours out speech, and night to night reveals knowledge. There is no speech, nor are there words, whose voice is not heard. Their voice goes out through all the earth, and their words to the end of the world. (Psalm 19:1-4)

David, along with the masses throughout history, examined creation and thought of the Creator. Some notable individuals who studied the natural order and recognized a creator were Albert Einstein, Arthur Compton, Blaise Pascal, Francis Bacon, Erwin Schrödinger, Sir Isaac Newton, Johannes Kepler, Nicolaus Copernicus, Anselm, and Plantinga — just to name a few. French biologist Louis Pasteur, who brought us the basic principles of vaccination, microbial fermentation, and pasteurization, actually believed studying science brought humanity nearer to God rather than farther from him. Though some would have us believe that science and faith are enemies, examining both the philosophical and observable evidence points us to a Creator.

In searching for evidence, we could start with classic cosmological arguments like William Lane Craig's work on the Kalam cosmological argument. Craig argues that anything that comes into being was caused by an external force — including the universe. We could examine transcendental arguments for God by thinkers like Immanuel Kant, who espoused the notion that the existence of a standard for morality and justice presuppose the existence of God. We could also look at the classic design argument, made famous by William Paley. Paley argues that anyone who carefully examines a wrist watch instinctively knows that it had to be designed. He uses that example to explain that human intelligence necessarily recognizes the intricacies of nature and its intentional patterns.

In addition to vast philosophical evidence, when we consider observable evidence in fields such as biochemistry and astronomy, we find overwhelming data in favor of design. After viewing the 'Red Shift' with Edwin Hubble, Einstein observed, "I now see the necessity of a beginning." Einstein and Hubble looked at the physical evidence and found that there was a point when the universe began to exist.

More observable evidence? The irreducible complexity (necessity of all present parts to function) of the human body: Cilia, blood clotting, the eye. Darwin himself was very aware of the complexities of the eye and discussed the evolutionary problems the eye presents in a section of *Origin of Species* titled, 'Organs of extreme perfection and complication.' If the human eye already casts doubt on the possibility of large scale evolution, what do scientists do with these fun questions: which came first, male or female? Which came first, digestive juices or the body's ability to resist their deteriorative affects? Or the classic, which came first the chicken or the egg? On the surface these may seem like sarcastic questions, but they reveal giant holes in the theories of macroevolution.

Other observable arguments for the created universe explore the remarkable fine tuning of natural systems. Research indicates that the universe was tuned like a radio dial to the exact specifications for life. If these universal parameters had been off only slightly, the entire cosmos could not exist. I'll list just a few that might leave your head spinning:

1. If the gravitational constant had been off by 1 part in $10^{40}$, the sun, which we need to live, would not exist; therefore, we would not exist. If neutrons were not 1.001 times the mass of protons, all protons would become neutrons or vice versa, and life would not exist.

2. If the cosmological constant varied by 1 part in $10^{120}$ the universe would either expand too rapidly and explode, or expand too slowly and implode.

3. If the electromagnetic force or the strong nuclear force varied slightly from their set parameters, life would be impossible.

4. If mass and energy of the universe were not
   evenly distributed precisely to 1 part in $10^{10}$
   123 we would not exist.[1]

How could such precision be the result of chance? It seems much more plausible to believe that these parameters were set by intelligence. It has been the conclusion of many intelligent thinkers throughout the centuries that the universe was designed.

When we look collectively at the philosophical proofs and the observable data concerning the natural display before us, it is easy to say with physicist Paul Davies, "the impression of design is overwhelming." All of the evidence of the universe shouts design. It seems surprisingly ignorant to disregard this solid evidence of design to cling to a theory that cannot account for the complexity of the eye, let alone the complexities of human emotion and consciousness.

# CATEGORY: GOD

When we allow ourselves to accept the overwhelming evidence of design, we are obligated to consider the Designer. What kind of creature or being could have single handedly created everything from itself? What type of intellect must one contain to orchestrate the symphony of the universe? What age must this being have to create all universes, which we cannot live to see, and still remain?

The answer, simply, is a Great Being. A Designer beyond the fathom of measurement and beyond human reason. Science is of no more use in describing the creator than is a painting in revealing the painter — perhaps other than the level of skill and intellect. It would only be possible to know of the painter what she left for us to read or maybe a secondary description should someone have known her personally. Concerning the Creator of the cosmos, the Bible declares that it is the very revelation and continued revealing of God. In this book, he reveals his plans, purposes, ends, means, and most importantly, his identity. As we have seen, the Bible proves that its words are true. In light of this fact, it is logical to conclude that the words revealing the identity of its Author are true as well.

*In the beginning, God,* the Bible pronounces. A fitting beginning to such an excellent creation. For if an eternal, necessary being existed before anything else, it is easy to believe that he then created. When we think of creating, we often think of getting our hands dirty. We imagine taking some substance or space and transforming it with our hands. We call that process 'creating,' but we are only using what already *is* and reforming or shaping that existing object. When God creates, He doesn't use material that already exists, or even hands, he just speaks. That's remarkable. I mean that in every sense of the word. Mark and re-mark the fact that God only speaks to create. His tongue is a forge and his words carpenters. He does not take from what we know to create, like matter and space. God takes the bottle of his own essence and pours out everything that does not yet exist into existence.

When God speaks, things happen. Ten times God speaks in Genesis 1 and the sum total of this 'Decalogue' is everything we know. Black holes, galaxies, tides, trees, the birds and the bees, all spoken by and from God. *Wait, you're telling me God could produce matter from nothing?* No, nothing comes from nothing. God created everything from himself. I want to explore just how this is possible by examining the identity of God.

Did you ever have a nickname? Or did you know someone who had a nickname? Most likely the person was nicknamed because of a characteristic, a quirk, or something they did. Like the kid from The Sandlot who had big glasses and squinted to see correctly, nicknamed 'Squints.' Sometimes the names are sarcastic like 'Jr.' referring to a 6'5" 350lb man. Or maybe you had a car that just wouldn't die that you called 'Ole Faithful.' These nicknames are given to characterize a person or thing. They tell us something about who they are.

God has revealed himself by several names, and the Bible refers to God with a few 'nicknames' based on his nature: the King of Kings, Lord of Lords, Lord of Hosts, Ancient of Days, Father/Abba, Most High, Elohim, El-Shaddai, Jehovah, Adonai.

Other names for God were given based upon what he did. Like YHWH-Yireh — "The Lord will provide" from Abraham in Genesis 22:13-14; YHWH-Rapha — "The Lord that heals" given by God himself in Exodus 15:26; YHWH-Nissi — "The Lord our Banner" from Moses in Exodus 17:8-15; YHWH-Shalom — "The Lord our Peace" from Gideon in Judges 6:24; YHWH-Ra-ah — "The Lord my Shepherd" from David in Psalm 23:1; YHWH-Tsid-kenu — "The Lord our Righteousness" from the prophet Jeremiah in Jeremiah 23:6, and YHWH-Shammah — "The Lord is present" from Ezekiel 48:35.

All of the names listed above include the name YHWH (יהוה), which is translated 'The LORD.' God himself used this name to reveal his own nature to Moses in Exodus 3. This name tells us everything about God. When God called Moses to lead his children out of Israel, Moses balked. "But...who shall I tell them sent me?" he managed. God replied in a very unusual manner. When you ask someone their name, they do not usually reply by stating the nature of their being. If you asked a bodybuilder his name, and he told you his name was 'Strength,' you would find it odd. In saying this, the bodybuilder would be stating that he *is* strength, literally, and the beginning and end of strength, onto-logically. We would find his claim absolutely crazy. It is not fitting for a human, or any finite being, to say they are the totality of an attribute like beauty or strength or wisdom, because they have only received these attributes from a source.

On the other hand, when God gives His name, he doesn't just say that he is an attribute. He simply says that he IS. He says to Moses "Ehyeh-asher-ehyeh" (אֶהְיֶה אֲשֶׁר אֶהְיֶה) "I Am who I AM," or I Will Be what I Will Be." This is amazing!

> God said to Moses, "I Am who I AM." And he said, "Say this to the people of Israel, 'I AM has sent me to you.'" God also said to Moses, "Say this to the people of Israel, 'The LORD, the God of your fathers, the God of Abraham, the God of Isaac, and the God of Jacob, has sent me to you.' This is my name forever, and thus I am to be remembered throughout all generations."
> (Ex. 3:14-15)

God is a verb? God is a noun? God is existence? God is existing? He is being? He is personhood? He is person? God says to Moses that he IS. Always existing, never caused, and never changing. No beginning, no end, no limit, no restriction, no category, no apology. There is no attribute which defines God; rather, his being defines all attributes. God is essentially saying he is complete in himself. He needs no one to exist. He needs nothing to complete or uphold him. He is not even self-caused, He IS. He is completely other. Awesome.

Humanity knows nothing like him. Anything strong, he is stronger. Anything beautiful, he is lovelier. Anything wise, his foolishness is wiser. He himself is the source of all excellence and wonder. Beauty finds its definition in him, and power learned its might from him. It is no surprise that God says, "Be still and know that I am God." When we sit down to fathom the God who IS, our knees should knock and our minds should fill with awe, for God IS.

# HOLY

There is a word that defines God. The word is used by God in Leviticus 20:26. The word? Holy. Literally, the word holy means 'a cut above', 'set apart', 'other'. If you aren't really understanding how to categorize God, you are getting it. He is his own category. He IS, unlike anything we know. God himself declares his holiness:

> I am the LORD, and there is no other; besides Me there is no God. (Isaiah 45:5)

> Remember the former things long past, for I am God, and there is no other; I am God, and there is no one like me. (Isaiah 46:9)

> For who is God, but the LORD? And who is a rock, except our God? (Psalm 18:31)

> For I the Lord do not change; therefore you, O children of Jacob, are not consumed. (Malachi 3:6)

God's holiness means that God is not like any other power, spiritual or physical. We can't even say that God is greater than a man the way a man is greater than a mouse or a mountain is greater than a molehill. Men, mice, mountains, and molehills all have something in common: limit. God has no limit. No beginning or end. He IS. There is never a moment God has not been. His attributes have no comparison.

Where does that leave us? The Bible reveals that we are like God, yet nothing like him. We bear the 'imago dei' or the 'image of God.' Think of a man casting a bronze image of himself. The bronze image bears a resemblance of the man but is nothing like the man. The image has no mind or flesh or joy like a man;

the image is in a category far below that of a man, but it bears the man's image. Similarly, we bear the image of God — we have the capacity to love, enjoy, think, and exist — but, we remain in a category far separate from his nature. We die, God cannot die. We make mistakes, God cannot make mistakes. We lie, God is the Truth. We are like him, but at the same time not at all like him. Consider a few examples with me.

Humans can have strength because God is strong, and we bear his image. But they can't possess God-strength. Imagine a son who is weaker than his father. Working hard to develop his muscles, he may grow to be stronger than his dad. He might grow capable of lifting a car — maybe even a bulldozer! But he cannot make the earth stop rotating on its axis and the moon stop orbiting the earth. All of the humans in all the world, with all of their strength and resources combined can't stop the earth from spinning. God can because his strength is holy (Joshua 10:13).

Men and women have the intelligence to perform medical procedures and save lives because God is intelligent, and we bear his image. But they can't raise someone from the dead or tell a disease to leave like an unwanted guest (Luke 8:44). God can because his power is holy (John 11:33-34).

People can hurt or empower with their words because God's words have power, and we bear his image. But human words can't stop a storm. God can because his words are holy (Mark 4:39). God is awful. Meaning, literally, full of awe. God is beyond imagining. Just a glimpse of God would allow you to understand his greatness and leave you astounded. (Is. 6:5; Job 42:5-6) Moses only saw the 'back' of God and his face was radiating so brightly that people could not look at him. (Ex. 33:20, 34:29) God is completely other.

Understanding just how far beyond the categories of human reason God is allows us to begin to comprehend how God alone created all that is. He is the only one who had the power to create. He is the only one who had the wisdom to make it perfect. In that creation, God did not merely apply an impersonal force. He created with His very own Word. That seems like hyperbole or a play on words, but it is not. The Word of God, 'logos', is best translated as the 'divine reason.' The apostle John speaks poetically of the origin of the cosmos:

> In the beginning was the Word, and the Word was with God, and the Word was God. He was in the beginning with God. All things were made through him, and without him was not anything made that was made. In him was life, and the life was the light of men. The light shines in the darkness, and the darkness has not overcome it.
> (John 1:1-5)

The Word — or the 'divine reason' — of God was the force which spoke all of creation into existence. Every molecule and mountain was formed by the Word of God. It seems very fitting that, on earth, Jesus of Nazareth was a carpenter. The Bible declares unapologetically that Jesus didn't just make great furniture, he made everything. John reveals again in 1 John:

> That which was from the beginning, which we have heard, which we have seen with our eyes, which we looked upon and have touched with our hands, concerning the word of life—the life was made manifest, and we have seen it, and testify to it and proclaim to you the eternal life, which was with the Father and was made manifest to us—that which we have seen and heard we proclaim also to you, so that you too may have fellowship with us; and indeed our fellowship is with the Father and his Son Jesus Christ.
> (1 John 1: 1-3)

This Word that was spoken was the overflow of the 'word of life' as John says above. What power, right? The Word of God speaks from his eternal self and creates angels and angles, stars and starfish. Jesus — the Word, the divine reason of God, eternal with God — created all things and then became a man that he would not just bear, but *be* the image of the invisible God.

> He is the image of the invisible God, the firstborn of all creation. For by him all things were created, in heaven and on earth, visible and invisible, whether thrones or dominions or rulers or authorities—all things were created through him and for him. And he is before all things, and in him all things hold together. And he is the head of the body, the church. He is the beginning, the firstborn from the dead, that in everything he might be preeminent. For in him all the fullness of God was pleased to dwell, and through him to reconcile to himself all things, whether on earth or in heaven, making peace by the blood of his cross. (Colossians 1:15-20)

Jesus is not a God among gods. He is the only one. He is completely different, holy, beyond comprehension. He has no equal. The power of Jesus Christ is not talked about enough. The grace of Jesus Christ is talked about a lot. But, do you know what the grace of Jesus Christ reveals the most? His power. I mean, let's be honest, telling a storm to calm down? Impressive (Mark 4:39). Walking on water like it's a sidewalk? Impressive (Matthew 14:25). Telling a man who was dead for four days to get up like a lazy teenage from the couch? Impressive. Feeding several thousand people with essentially a few Lunchables? Impressive. But what is most impressive is that Jesus forgives sins.

*Well, he just forgives sins because he's a nice guy,* you might think. *What's so impressive about that?* It's impressive because *only* Jesus can forgive sins. Jesus forgives sin because he has the power and authority to do so (Matthew 9:6). No one else can do this because no one else is God. Only God can forgive sins because God is the one who is ultimately sinned against. I can't forgive someone for throwing a stone through my neighbor's window. Only my neighbor can forgive the felon. Only God can ultimately forgive, because even when we sin against other people, we are sinning ultimately against God (Psalm 51:4).

Sinning against the same Great Being that we were talking about before. The God who is bigger, and faster, and stronger — this is Jesus. Demons know the power of Jesus. Whenever they come in contact with Jesus, there is never a struggle for authority. Demons always talk to Jesus like a conquered enemy speaks to their conqueror. Demons approach Jesus with a white flag, not a battle cry. In Luke 8, we see an example of their submission toward Jesus and his power and authority over them:

> Jesus then asked him, "What is your name?" And he said, "Legion," for many demons had entered him. And they begged him not to command them to depart into the abyss. Now a large herd of pigs was feeding there on the hillside, and they begged him to let them enter these. So he gave them permission. (Luke 8:30-32)

It is interesting that demons dialogue with Jesus like a lamb pleading with a lion. If Jesus was in a power struggle with demons they would not be 'begging' for mercy. If Jesus was not the most powerful being, demons would not need Jesus' 'permission.' Demons know who Jesus is; they have always known. Scripture records that Jesus cast demons out of people and the demons cried that Jesus was the Messiah. Demons know Jesus is Boss.

"Ha! What have you to do with us, Jesus of Nazareth? Have you come to destroy us? I know who you are—the Holy One of God." But Jesus rebuked him, saying, "Be silent and come out of him!" And when the demon had thrown him down in their midst, he came out of him, having done him no harm. And they were all amazed and said to one another, "What is this word? For with authority and power he commands the unclean spirits, and they come out!" (Luke 4:34-36)

And demons also came out of many, crying, "You are the Son of God!" But he rebuked them and would not allow them to speak, because they knew that he was the Christ. (Luke 4:41)

And he healed many who were sick with various diseases, and cast out many demons. And he would not permit the demons to speak, because they knew him. (Mark 1:34)

Jesus of Nazareth is the Word of God who spoke all of creation into existence. He is the power which is beyond measure on the Richter scale. Earthquakes are not a result of God walking or jumping. Earthquakes are God laughing that we think his footsteps would be so weak. He is the all-time, undisputed, undefeated, God.

# PERFECTION

Jesus is not only powerful, but also perfect (Luke 18:19; Matthew 5:48). His very essence is perfection. God knows all and exists outside of time. It is impossible that God could make a mistake. He had seen all worlds before they were created. Not only was it impossible to create imperfection from perfection, it was impossible for Jesus to create a wrong end for he had seen and spoken all ends before their beginning (Isaiah 46:10).

When God created, he created perfectly. *Wait, doesn't the Bible say that what God created was good and not perfect?* It does, but there is no difference. We have to define our terms before we can understand what 'good' means. When someone uses the term 'good' they usually mean it in a sense of graduation (i.e. good, better, best). You have probably received a paper back from a teacher that said, "Good Job" or "Good Effort" with a B slapped on the top when you were hoping for "Excellent." In the English language, 'good' is usually used as a gentle adjective to say, "It could be better."

God doesn't use the word 'good' in that sense. When God says something is good, he is saying it is lacking bad. No bad, only good. Only good, therefore perfect. If there is no bad, there is only perfection. 'Good' in God's vocabulary means *cannot be any better*. To say that something could be better is to say that the object is not perfect, and if it isn't perfect, it could have more good. If something can have more good, it is deficient; therefore, it is not good. In God's vocabulary, there is only perfect and not-perfect (Good and bad). God is the standard of good. He is the only one who knows all possible worlds to know what is good.

In Genesis 1, God steps back from his creation and states that it is 'good' (Genesis 1:3, 10, 12, 18, 21, 25, 31). Perfect. It contains only good and no bad. God is essentially saying, "It cannot get any better than this." When God created, there was no disease, there was no evil, there was no mistake. Adam and Eve: perfect. Death: unknown. No tragedy, only comedy. God can only make good things because he is only good. Thinking God can create bad is like believing that you can pour orange juice from a sealed bottle of Coca-Cola. You can only pour out what the bottle contains.

But, what about all the death, and disease and evil that is in the world today? Where did all of this come from if what God made was perfect? If God only creates what is good, who creates all the bad? Those questions will be answered, but before we go running off to put God in the stocks, let's not forget how awesome he is. He IS; perfect and powerful. Knowledge? He literally wrote the book. No one is sneaking up on God, and no one is going to stop him or get in the way of his plans. He can't be beaten, and he can't be outsmarted. He speaks with power and authority, and creation cannot help but stop and listen.

# ORIGIN 2.0

*The beginning of man's rebellion against God, was, and is, the lack of a thankful heart.*

**FRANCIS SCHAEFFER**

*There is no distinction, for all have sinned and fall short of the glory of God*

**THE APOSTLE PAUL**

*If this cursed and fallen world*
*Holds such beauty as what I see,*
*Imagine the beauty of paradise*
*That's gladly waiting for me.*

**JOYCE RACHELLE**

*The unleashed power of the atom has changed everything save our modes of thinking, and thus we drift toward unparalleled catastrophe.*

**ALBERT EINSTEIN**

*I felt that I breathed an atmosphere of sorrow.*

**EDGAR ALLAN POE**

*No one sees anything funny in a tree falling down. No one sees a delicate absurdity in a stone falling down. No man stops in the road and roars with laughter at the sight of the snow coming down. The fall of roofs and high buildings is treated with some gravity. It is only when a man tumbles down that we laugh. Why do we laugh? Because it is a grave religious matter: it is the Fall of Man. Only man can be absurd: for only man can be dignified.*

**G.K. CHESTERTON**

# ORIGIN 2.0
## HOW DID WE GET HERE?

## UP OR DOWN

Have you ever walked into a room and thought, *why did I come in here, again?* Have you ever arrived at your destination, parked the car, and suddenly awoken to reality thinking, *wow, I don't even remember driving here*? Or maybe you are in a life situation that has left you thinking *how did I get in this mess?* It happens to all of us.

When we think about the beauty of creation that is described in Genesis and compare that paradise to our problems, we are left thinking *how did we get here?* I'm not talking about how the universe was created or how human beings were created. God created everything by the power of his Word. The question we are asking is *how did things go from bliss to brokenness?* How did we come to know a world that is mean? The answer to this question will lead us to an unlikely discovery: hope.

From an evolutionary worldview, it is assumed that humanity has evolved to reach a higher form of existence. Humans have evolved from low elements to high functioning animals. But this worldview hardly accounts for the ancient feeling inside our bones that humans contain a divine dignity. We inherently recognize the difference between a hamburger and man-burger. One is delightful with fries and a Coke — the other is difficult even to think about. Why? Perhaps because there remains in us traces of the eternal. The ruins of a divine imprint. Eternity is written on our hearts, Ecclesiastes 3 tells us. Have you ever wondered why selfies are so popular? Whether we realize it or not, there is something amazing in us to behold: the debris of the divine. However, far from evolving in a positive direction, the Bible displays the human condition as falling from the heights of immortality to death.

# DOWN

In the beginning, all was perfect. Adam and Eve shared a harmonious relationship both with one another and with all of creation. The narrative painted in Genesis 1 and 2 is a picture of pure paradise. In Eden there is no disease, no death, no lying, and no cheating. No bad, only good.

God created everything perfectly, including humans (I Timothy 4:4; Gen. 1:31). God formed Adam "of dust from the ground and breathed into his nostrils the breath of life, and the man became a living creature" (Gen. 2:7). Then he [God] "fashioned into a woman the rib which He had taken from the man, and brought her to the man" (Gen. 2:22; Matt. 19:4). God saw everything that he had made, and behold, it was "very good" (Gen.1:31). Everything was holy, and God was present.

We would expect the Bible to end here with *"And they lived happily ever after,"* but we know better. There are forty-eight other chapters in Genesis, and 65 other books in the whole story. This is far from the blissful end. We need only look at the evil in the world and read on to know something went very, very wrong.

Human nature tends to long for bygone days. We recognize the painful effects of time passing and seek to return to our former glory. The older generation speaks of 'the good old days when the world was right.' Women may seek to erase deepening lines and age spots with skins creams and concealer. Men might take supplements to strengthen a weakening body. Courtrooms are an arena to restore justice. War seeks to return a people to former days of peace, prosperity, or glory.

It's easy to find this pattern in human nature, but why? Where does it come from?

The pattern began in Eden. More specifically, in our *loss* of Eden. When Adam and Eve first sinned against God, they tried to cover themselves with fig leaves so that they might appear innocent before God. They weren't trying to create innocence they had never possessed; they were seeking to return to their *prior state* of right standing with God. With each technological advance throughout history, innovators have sought to improve our health, comfort, or quality of life. But, in Eden's paradise, humans had no fear of death, disease, or malnutrition. With each new cell phone model, we try to communicate more clearly. But, communication was perfect in Eden. Each new business venture seeks some form of joy, whether money or success or power. Joy was once full in Eden. Humans have always been pursuing a joy that they feel missing in the world. We miss it and seek it because it once belonged to us, and so we strive to find it again.

In this search, we must be careful. Many have imagined success, or knowledge, or relationships to hold true joy and have, achieving it, found it empty. Our souls still long for the beauty of Eden, but Eden has fallen. We may try to rebuild it, but it was made of elements we no longer possess.

The curtain of the fall in Genesis 3 opens with the description of a serpent "more crafty than any other beast of the field that the LORD had made." This Satan, as he is named, the tempter of humanity (Matt. 4:1; 1 Cor. 7:5; 2 Cor. 11:3; John 13:2; Rev. 12:9), the one who prowls around the whole earth like a "roaring lion, seeking someone to devour," (1 Peter 5:8) was the one who tempted Eve. He had fallen from glory, and misery loves company. He was once an angelic being, beautiful, and righteous. But, he fell. Pride grabbed him by the foot and pulled him to the lowest regions of Hell. Both Isaiah and Ezekiel speak of the fall of Satan from his glory:

> How you are fallen from heaven, O Day Star, son of Dawn! How you are cut to the ground, you who laid the nations low! You said in your heart, I will ascend to heaven; above the stars of God I will set my throne on high; I will sit on the mount of assembly in the far reaches of the north; I will ascend above the heights of the clouds; I will make myself like the Most high.' But you are brought down to Sheol, to the far reaches of the pit. (Isaiah 14:12-15)

> You were an anointed guardian cherub. I placed you; you were on the holy mountain of God; in the midst of the stones of fire you walked. You were blameless in your ways from the day you were created, till unrighteousness was found in you. In the abundance of your trade you were filled with violence in your midst, and you sinned; so I cast you as a profane thing from the mountain of God, and I destroyed you, O guardian cherub,

from the midst of the stones of fire. Your heart was proud because of your beauty; you corrupted your wisdom for the sake of your splendor. I cast you to the ground; I exposed you before kings, to feast their eyes on you. By the multitude of your iniquities, in the unrighteousness of your trade you profaned your sanctuaries; so I brought fire out from your midst; it consumed you, and I turned you to ashes on the earth in the sight of all who saw you. All who know you among the peoples are appalled at you; you have come to a dreadful end and shall be no more forever.
(Ezekiel 28:14-19)

Satan was once a beautiful cherub whose pride made him the first evil being. His very enticing proposition to Eve was that she would be "like God" (Gen. 3:5). What she did not know is that she was already as fully like God as a human could be. She could not die, she did not know pain nor any evil thing. Her beauty would never fade, and her heart would never be broken. But pride is not content; it wants what it can't have.

Satan tempted Eve with knowledge. He tried to convince her that she would not be complete until she indulged in the fruit of the Tree of Knowledge that God had forbidden them to eat. As she listened and grew discontent, she was about to enroll in the program of 'taking what doesn't belong to you' — the very one that had brought Satan down. This same program of pride ultimately brought down Eve, and then Adam, and with them the entire human race (Gen. 3:6; Rom. 5:12). In a moment, Adam and Eve knew something entirely new: shame. Since that eternal tremor we have all felt the same.

I believe that the fruit tasted lovely, but not nearly as lovely as the two had hoped. Immediately, the taste of remorse and fear choked out any hints of pleasure as Adam and Eve began the eternal struggle of trying to return to their former innocence. Desperately, Adam and Eve tried to hide their shame by sewing loincloths to cover their most sacred parts and to mask their fear. The art of covering up dawned on that day.

Sin, or 'cosmic treason' as the late R.C. Sproul coined it, had entered the world through Adam's sin, and all that was beautiful fell apart like a cracked mirror slowly splintering into pieces (Rom. 5:12; 1 Cor. 15:21). Adam's work was cursed, Eve's pain was increased, relationship with God and man was broken, they were cast out of the paradise of Eden, death was given reign, and the whole universe was brought under a curse (Rom. 8:20). Yet even in this curse, God, in his powerful grace, promised hope (Gen. 3:15). God, in his mercy, had a plan to lift humanity up from the fall.

Immediately, in Genesis 4 the chaos begins to unfold. Cain kills Abel, the world dives into debauchery, and the whole earth is destroyed with a flood (Gen. 7). You can see the immortality that humans once bore in Eden begin to disappear like a vanishing fog. Look at the ages of the sons of Adam begin to decrease in Genesis 5. The average age of Adam's descendants to Noah is 857.5 years.[1] In Genesis 6, God sets the limit of human life to 120 years, and today the average lifespan is less than 80 years (Ps. 90:10).

Sin has caused humanity's former glory to wear out like a fine garment disintegrating into a rag. From Adam to the flood, the flood to Abraham, Abraham to Isaac, Isaac to Jacob, Jacob to Joseph, Joseph to Moses, Moses to Joshua, Joshua to the Judges, the Judges to the Kings, The Kings to the Prophets, the Prophets to the Exile, the Exile to the return from exile, the return from exile to the Roman empire and every moment since, the earth spirals farther and farther away from perfection and deeper into darkness.

Sin has left us in dire straits. Sin, which promised Eve life, only brought death, through Adam, to all. You and me and the flowers and the trees, all under the curse of sin. All under death (Rom. 5:12). Though Satan whispered gently in Eve's ear that death would not come, death ignited and consumed all.

Ephesians 2 tells us that as a result of our fall from former glory, we are all spiritually dead. Our spirits, according to Scripture, are without life. Because we are spiritually dead, we cannot understand spiritual things and we cannot please God (1 Cor. 2:14). We cannot please God because faith is necessary to please him, "for whoever would draw near to God must believe that he exists and that he rewards those who seek him" (Heb. 11:6). We have no ability to repent or trust in Christ on our own (John 6:44; John 6:65; Phil. 1:29; Eph. 2:8-9). We cannot obey God because our minds are hostile toward God, and we suppress the truth (Rom. 1:18, 8:6-8). We cannot see or enter the kingdom of heaven because we are not holy (John 3:3; Matt. 5:20; Rom. 3:10,23, 5:12).

Thus, we find ourselves in a predicament that we are not able to *will* ourselves out of. Just as the physically dead cannot do anything to change their situation, the spiritually dead are equally powerless to alter their status. The only way we could ever breathe spiritual life again is if it is God's will to save us. Thankfully, it was his plan from the foundation of the world not only to save but also to forgive.

# UP

Imagine you've just met a young couple who is expecting a child. There is likely a lot of joy and preparation in their home, and you can sense their excitement at welcoming a new life into their family. You look at them and consider the hardships of the world we live in and hope that they are prepared for what lies ahead. Later, you learn that the young couple is incredibly wealthy and has already begun to make great preparations for their child. They have a trust fund already containing millions of dollars set up for the child to receive at a certain age. They have prepared a room in their mansion just for the child and have every intention, and the means, to lavish good things upon that child. Now, you look at that woman's growing belly and think to yourself, *Man, kid, if only you knew the good plans that your parents have in store for you!*

We look at our present world and think, *what good could possibly be found here?* God looks at the broken world and thinks, *I have got great plans for you, kid!* God knew the human race was in a desperate situation. He is the Author of Life. He knows the End from the Beginning and all that is in between. He IS. Before Satan had fallen, before the cosmos was conceived, before Adam and Eve were exiled from Eden, God in his infinite self, had planned the salvation of the world.

The death of Jesus Christ on the cross for the forgiveness of sins was not a second-thought remedy to our problem. It was the will of God from the foundation of the world to deliver all who believe through Jesus Christ (Acts 2:23; I Peter 1:20; Rev. 13:8). The love of God for this broken world is a message succinctly stated by John: "For God so loved the world that he gave his only Son that whoever believes in him will not perish, but have everlasting life." Isaiah tells us that God's plan to save the world through Jesus was planned before Christ came:

> Yet it was the will of the LORD to crush him; he has put him to grief; when his soul makes an offering for guilt, he shall see his offspring; he shall prolong his days; the will of the LORD shall prosper in his hand. (Isaiah 53:10)

It is often said by people that God, if he exists, is not loving. "If he was loving," some say, "how could he let me to go through what I've gone through? How could God allow so much evil?" That question reveals the fact of our broken world. We will encounter the consequences of sin and feel the effects of death. But, we must remember who God is.

Is it appropriate to say that a father is not loving toward his children when he provides abundantly for them and seeks their good in all he does? It is even less fitting to say that a man is not loving toward his children when he lays down his life so his children might live. Likewise, it is inappropriate to say that God is not loving. God has not only purposed to love, he has loved in time and space.

God, in his love, made plans in his unsearchable mind, to lift his children up from the pit of death and clothe them with life. God, in his love, made the decree to forgive us — his enemies — and make us his friends. God, in his love, sent that which was most precious to him to redeem those who were not precious at all. "And love consists in this," John tells us, "not that we loved God, but that He loved us and sent His Son as an atoning sacrifice for our sins" (1 John 4:10). God, in his love, did not wait for humanity to become lovely, for he knew the day would never arrive. Instead, he decided to make those who were unlovely, lovely by the power of his grace. "God showed his love for us in that while we were still sinners, Christ died for us," Paul says (Rom.5:8). There is no greater love that a man can show for his friends than to lay down his life that they might live (John 15:13). It is a matter of fact that God loves — He actually died so we might finally live.

Someone may say, "God does not love me," but that statement simply isn't true. The speaker may not have *accepted* the love of God, but God has freely offered his love to all and sent his son to die on their behalf. The speaker may not *believe* in God or his love, but it is not the fault of God that the speaker does not believe. Humans may choose to believe any lie, but their choice is not the fault of God. No one will ever be able to stand before God and excuse himself saying, "I did not believe in you because I believed in evolution." God might reply, "Did I not leave you a fossil record devoid of transitional forms, which displays my instantaneous creative power? Did I not leave you my Word which proved to be true for all ages? (Luke 16:29) Did I not leave you with reason to understand the design of such wonderful order displayed in my creation?" Belief in God for lack of evidence is no argument before God. God's "invisible attributes, namely, his eternal power and divine nature, have been clearly perceived, ever since the creation of the world, in the things that have been made. So they [we] are without excuse." (Rom. 1:20). The evidence of God is all around us and in our own hearts and conscience.

Someone may say, "God may have created me, then, but God did not die for me!" Again, the speaker may have rejected the forgiveness offered in his death, but Jesus Christ "is the propitiation for our sins, and not for ours only but also for the sins of the whole world (1 John 2:2). Jesus has died for the sins of the whole world, every man, woman, and child. When Jesus bled upon the cross, the eternal sacrifice which dripped from those timbers was spilled once for all (Heb.10:1-18). It is untrue for anyone to say that God did not die for them. There are no generations or races or people groups beyond the forgiveness offered in Jesus, for "everyone who calls upon the name of the LORD will be saved" (Rom. 5:13). In that verse, we see that God has died for the forgiveness of everyone's sins, but not everyone's sins are forgiven. A person must repent from sin and believe in Christ, calling on his name, to be saved (Acts 2:38; Mark 1:15). Today, every person who repents and believes and receives the Spirit will be saved.

Someone may say, "But God is not just to require everyone to repent! What about an innocent boy or girl in the heart of

Motuo? Surely it is not kind to require their repentance." Here, the speaker attempts to corner God using his own just nature against him. But God's justice is so complete that he cannot bear sin in his presence. All humans are without hope in their own strength. We have been cut from defiled clay; every part of our beings needs to be washed clean.

Consider a child. No parent has to teach their children to be selfish or to lie, steal, or cheat. Those who are born of the human race are born in sin and are in need of salvation: "There is no one righteous, not even one" (Rom. 3:10; Ps. 14:4; 1 John 1:8). It is the kindness of God that leads us to repentance, not his anger. God desires that people be saved and rejoices in their repentance (Rom. 2:4; Luke 15:7; Eccles. 7:20). He commands us to repent because he loves. He forgives because he is merciful. He is merciful because he is holy. It is merciful that God commands repentance; without it we would stay forever locked in the prison of our fallen state.

Someone may say, "Even if God was so loving, if he was God, he could have created a world without evil! Maybe God wasn't powerful enough to prevent evil! Or maybe he's not kind at all!" Here, the speaker shows a lack of understanding of God's nature. God is Wisdom. It is not our place to tell an author how to write a story, for it is their own. J.R.R. Tolkien was not bombard-ed with hate mail for creating Orcs in the world of Middle Earth. He created them so they would be destroyed. Did he not create them with the purpose of proving the power and purpose of good over evil? We rejoice when they are cut down, we do not protest. We delight that Sauron was created because it is the greatest joy of Middle Earth to watch him fall in destruction and the rightful and good king to be crowned. If we don't mistrust Tolkien in the middle of his tale, how much more should we trust the God who IS Wisdom as we live out his story.

In our own joy over the destruction of fictitious evil, we must acknowledge that we approve of the justice of God and his final destruction of evil. It is not that the people of Middle Earth exist and feel joy — they have no existence. Rather, we feel joy. Tolkien wove the elements of evil and good, and the tension of their warring, as an allegory of our own existence. Every fantastic world created reminds us of the power of God to animate his world with his imagination and set it in motion like a movie script comes to life on a screen. Every character in reality has been cast by God. Every character has its purpose.

Evil is cast in God's drama as a pawn. Evil is not in competition with him. The entire drama of human existence was penned before time began (Isaiah 14:27, 46:10; Heb. 6:17; Ps. 33:11). Like an author who pours over his story time and again before he releases it, God in his eternity created his story in perfection before he set it in motion. We experience reality as if we are watching in unfold for the first time. God watches reality as a rerun that he has seen for all of eternity. Because he contains only good, all that has come from God is good. Evil itself is not good. Evil works for the good purposes of God in a way similar to the way that Sauron, while evil, is created and used for the good purpose of the glory of *The Lord of the Rings*. J.R.R. Tolkien is not declared to be evil for using evil in his story. Neither is God evil for using evil for the glory of his story and the majesty of his Name. God exists separately from evil in his goodness and uses evil for good ends.

For God's own glory he allows evil and makes it accomplish his own purposes. Evil is not existing without God's knowledge or his permission. Evil spirits ask Jesus for permission, remember? Throughout the Bible, we see God's sovereignty over all things, including evil, working for his good purposes. But the greatest display of God's use of evil for his good purpose is in the narrative of Jesus Christ, God's own Son who was killed by evil.

As John Piper says, "God did not just overcome evil at the cross. He made evil serve the overcoming of evil. He made evil commit suicide in doing its worst evil." Evil crushed Jesus so Jesus could crush evil. The Bible immaculately displays Gods use of the evil of the cross to display God's glory:

> He will swallow up death forever; and the Lord GOD will wipe away tears from all faces, and the reproach of his people he will take away from all the earth, for the LORD has spoken. (Isaiah 25:8)

> ...In order to make known the riches of his glory for vessels of mercy, which he has prepared beforehand for glory. (Romans 9:23)

> When the perishable puts on the imperishable, and the mortal puts on immortality, then shall come to pass the saying that is written: "Death is swallowed up in victory." "O death, where is your victory? O death, where is your sting?" The sting of death is sin, and the power of sin is the law. But thanks be to God, who gives us the victory through our Lord Jesus Christ.
> (1 Corinthians 15:54-56)

> Since therefore the children share in flesh and blood, he himself likewise partook of the same things, that through death he might destroy the one who has the power of death, that is, the devil... (Hebrews 2:14)

> And now He has revealed this grace through the appearing of our Savior, Christ Jesus, who has abolished death and illuminated the way to life and immortality through the gospel...
> (2 Timothy 1:10)

And the devil who had deceived them was thrown into the lake of fire and sulfur, into which the beast and the false prophet had already been thrown. There they will be tormented day and night forever and ever. (Revelation 20:10)

Then Death and Hades were thrown into the lake of fire. This is the second death – the lake of fire. (Revelation 20:14)

Does it sound like evil is hiding behind God's back thwarting his purposes? If God used evil to glorify his name through the humiliation of his perfect son through death on a cross, how much more will God use evil in our own lives to work for good? "Truly God works all things together for the good of those who love Him, who are called according to His purpose" (Rom. 8:28).

Remember how God gained glory through the liberation of his people from Pharaoh. Remember how Joseph suffered as a prisoner and slave before he was raised to second in command in Pharaoh's household and used to save God's children from famine. Remember the captivity of Daniel, Shadrach, Meshach and Abednego and God's plan to reveal himself to their captor Nebuchadnezzar. Look at Jonah and Nineveh, Lot and Sodom and Gomorrah, and even the woman caught in adultery. These all, in harmony, shout that God uses evil for his glory. Evil is by no means a mistake; it is a means to ensure that we cannot mistake the power and glory of God over it.

# ALIVE

We have seen God's power over evil. We have seen our powerless condition — our inability to restore our former God-given glory. Our spiritual deadness. In his mercy, Jesus saw it, too, and stepped down from heaven to raise us up from death to life.

Born of the Virgin Mary, through the miraculous conception recorded in Luke 1, Jesus came to earth like Adam, a man, so he could save humanity. Hebrews 2:17 tells us that "He had to be made like His brothers in every way, that He might become a merciful and faithful high priest in service to God, in order to make atonement for the sins of the people." In other words, since God's justice necessitates payment for human sins, Jesus had to become human to make that payment on our behalf.

Paul makes the point explicitly clear that Jesus did not have to die for his own sake because Jesus lived his whole life without sin. Though he was fully man, he was also fully God. As a result, he had the power to resist every temptation and always do the right thing in every situation. Thus, in his death, he took our sins upon himself to pay the penalty for them. Paul says it this way: "For our sake he made him to be sin who knew no sin, so that in him we might become the righteousness of God" (2 Cor. 5:21). When Jesus, the very Word of God who spoke the world into being, died upon the cross, his holy and eternal blood forever made a sacrifice for sin (Heb. 9:22). Jesus' sacrificial death made peace with God possible for us (Eph. 2:15). However, it was Jesus' resurrection that killed death and made immortality a reality again.

God, like a mighty king of old, threw off his crown and entered the fray. He saw the death of his people and strapped a sword to his thigh and thundered into battle on a white horse. Yet, he let his enemy take him in exchange for his people and shed his blood that his people would be ransomed. And then, in his power, he rose from the grave.

This is precisely why Jesus died; he was the only one who had the power to slay death and rise to life again. God's power is beyond the limits of death. Even though we see all things die, there is a power greater than death. Hope for humanity sprung from the ground on that first Easter morning. Jesus rose from the grave because his power is greater. As Tolkien's stroke of pen brought Sauron tumbling to destruction, so the pen of God wrote the destruction of death with ease. Paul, preaching at Pentecost, declares the power of Jesus over death, saying:

> This Jesus, delivered up according to the definite plan and foreknowledge of God, you crucified and killed by the hands of lawless men. God raised him up, loosing the pangs of death, because it was not possible for him to be held by it. (Acts 2:23-24)

The human race now knows two strains: Dead and Living — Adam and Christ. Everyone born in Adam dies. All who are born in Christ live forever, for they are given the same Spirit of power that raised Jesus from the dead, which cannot die. "If the Spirit of him who raised Jesus from the dead dwells in you," Paul said, "he who raised Christ Jesus from the dead will also give life to your mortal bodies through his Spirit who dwells in you" (Rom. 8:11). Humans have been dignified again. We have been made immortal in Christ.

All who repent and believe in Christ for salvation are given forgiveness and the resurrecting power of God. They are made into a new creature (2 Cor. 5:17). They have not only been forgiven, their shame erased; they have also been brought up to heaven and crowned with eternal life. We have not slowly evolved into better creatures. In a moment, the power of God has created a new human race, born of God, born in power, alive forever.

# IDENTITY

East or west, north or south, ancient or modern, the problem is the same
and the solution is the same. Once we understand the heinousness of sin, we
will gain a deep and lasting gratitude for God.

**RAVI ZACHARIAS**


No one is good except God alone.

**JESUS**


I once was dead in sin, alone and hopeless
A child of wrath I walked, condemned in darkness
But Your mercy brought new life
And in Your love and kindness
Raised me up with Christ, and made me righteous

**CITIZENS AND SAINTS**


Men in general are quick to believe that which
they wish to be true.

**JULIUS CAESAR**


When Satan tells me I am a sinner he comforts me immeasurably, since
Christ died for sinners.

**MARTIN LUTHER**


God creates out of nothing. Wonderful you say. Yes, to be sure, but he does
what is still more wonderful: He makes saints out of sinners.

**SØREN KIERKEGAARD**

# IDENTITY
## RICH KIDS

## SHARK ATTACK

Have you ever seen a great white shark attack a fur seal? It is fierce! *Planet Earth*, BBC's dazzling display of the glory of creation, captures this breathtaking moment in slow motion. An immensely terrifying great white shark goes completely airborne in the attack. Frame by frame you watch in wonder as the shark's jaws slowly close like an iron trap, marking the final chapter of the seal's life. The wonder and the treacherous nature of the ocean world splashes into your living room. You become an eyewitness of a terrific and powerful display of nature.

But the BBC does not notify the police. Local and national news stations are not informed. There has been a vicious attack upon life, but no one alerts the authorities. This is because there has been no law broken. When a shark attacks a fur seal he is not breaking a law, moral or otherwise. He is simply fulfilling his natural purpose of being a shark. Eating seals is what sharks do. Think how humorous it would be if a man called a local police officer to report the murder of a fur seal by a shark. If he was calling in jest, we would find it funny. If he was emphatic that a true murder had been committed we would think the man confused about the true meaning of the term 'murder' and the true nature of animals.

If, however, a shark attacks a human being, it is a different ballgame. The authorities are called, and local and national news channels cover the tragedy. We all gasp because an immortal has been viciously attacked. We are appalled because one bearing the image of God has been battered by a beast. When human blood is spilled, we all tremble, for the life of our ancient brother is spilling out upon the ground.

Humanity is made in the image of God and bears a mark of divinity that no other species enjoys. Only humans pause to look in the mirror and marvel at the signs of aging. Only humans make remarks about the passing of time like it is a novelty. Only humans suffer from disease and consciously hate is effects, for they see it is destroying something beautiful. Only humans suffer and wonder how such a wretched event could happen to them. Only humans seek to shield the innocence of their children from the moral evil that pervades culture. Animals do not sit and ponder the meaning of their life. Humans see these events as unusual because the eternal nature of our soul remembers the former days of our immortal glory in Eden. Our identity as human beings revolves, as the earth circles the sun, around the impression that we are sacred. We cannot escape the notion that we are precious.

In addition to the evidence found in our own experiences, God's Word speaks clearly about the eternal imprint of humans and the value of our souls. When God spoke his law to Moses at Mt. Sinai, he decreed a code for valuing human life that even non-believers would hold true: don't murder another human, don't take the possessions of another human, don't testify falsely about another human, don't commit adultery with another human (Ex. 20).

The Ten Commandments can make people think that God is only about rules and regulations and stealing our joy. Far from stealing our joy, the Ten Commandments were given to increase our joy. The Ten Commandments were given to protect the sacred nature of humanity from defilement. These decrees unapologetically reveal that men and women are valuable.

In our fallen condition, God gave rules to men and women so that they would not steal the joy He gave to every human being. When a man steals from us, it robs us not only of the item taken, but primarily of our dignity. When someone steals from us, our joy is pickpocketed. When adultery is committed, the guilty party steals the honor and the purity of the union of marriage.

The laws which we find written in Scripture declare that the human race is sacred. However, they speak also of God's demand to be worshipped. No other gods beside him. No idolatry. These commands are only fitting. There is no other being who is worthy of worship. There is no other being who is holy. There is no other God who IS. God also commands the worship of himself for our own joy.

When a child is young, he pursues certain ends because he believes they will bring him the most joy. He might try to be the best at his craft, to be the strongest in the gym, to win the heart of the loveliest woman, or to make the most money. To achieve what he imagines will bring him the most happiness, he may lie, steal, cheat and forsake friends. Even though he may become the strongest or make the most money, he will forsake greater ends. He will forsake honor and love and faithfulness. He will find his honor ruined in his pursuit of lesser ends. In his misguided attempt to become more, he will have become less. His sacred soul will have become tainted because he has worshiped an idol.

It is the same with all of humanity. When we make anything less than God our end, we destroy our dignity. One might say, "I will not worship God, but rather myself and therefore increase my dignity." In the worship of himself, the speaker might lie and steal and cheat. But, in time, the soul who seeks to ascribe worth to itself will not feel itself dignified — but rather ruined. It will not feel like a God — but rather a wretch.

Only in the true worship of God do we find our highest joy and dignity. In worshipping God alone, we pledge our allegiance to the greatest being. We understand our identity as his children — sons and daughters of the only King. We recognize the divine ethic that has been written on our hearts. We aim our affections and delight to the only worthy One. Miraculously, when we have ultimate love for God, we have the highest love for humanity and the highest dignity for ourselves.

## POOR KIDS

Country music singer Luke Bryan sings, "I believe this world ain't half as bad as it looks...I believe most people are good," as we nod our heads to the familiar beat. The idea that humans are inherently good doesn't just slip into the occasional country tune — it pervades our culture. It's easy to understand why. Popular language confuses the term by setting 'good' at the low end of the graduation spectrum of good-better-best. 'Good' is considered average or passable — "well, at least I'm not a murderer. I'm basically good, right?"

Herein lies the confusion. When people say that humans are inherently good, they mean that we contain more good than bad. They are saying that at the core of a person's soul is a desire for good, but a lot of bad gets in the way. No one describes people as perfect. Few would dare to say this even of themselves. "But people can still be 'good' without being *perfect*, right?" It's a tempting philosophy to adopt among a culture that's uncomfortable with absolutes. But, before we climb aboard the "people are basically good" train, we must pause to remember what 'good' really means. By definition, 'good' means the *absence* of bad.

If even one tiny plop of cow poop falls into your cookie batter, you will have bad cookies. Even though the proportion of good seemingly outweighs the bad, the whole batch is ruined. Similarly, anything or anyone that contains even a trace of evil or 'badness' is effectively defiled and cannot possibly be good. According to God's standard, unless something is perfect, it is not good. Remember God's declaration over creation? "It is good" — absent of bad — and, therefore, perfect. To God, 'good' and 'perfect' are synonymous.

When humans try to define 'good' for themselves, chaos ensues. One person says that X-amount of goodness makes someone a good person. But someone else has another standard entirely. If we look to ourselves, we will never find a solid point of reference — the carrot will always be in front of the donkey's nose. Yet, there is an external, eternal standard of goodness that our conscience recognizes. We inherently understand the ideas of good and bad, right and wrong, and 'do unto others'. We know when we — or others — have fallen short of that standard. The very fact that we admit our imperfection gives our conscience away. We are not perfect. We contain 'badness'. Thus, our conscience acknowledges that good is neither defined by humanity nor culture, nor nations, nor themselves. Good is what God is.

God is the unmoving, all-knowing, perfect standard of good. Good learned its manners from him, and the law looked to him for its directions. If God does not hold the standards of good then there is no standard at all. As Dostoevsky said, "If God does not exist, then everything is permitted." But God does exist, and his laws exist. His law, emanating from his goodness, is the ultimate standard of good. This law unveils the sacred nature of humanity. God has not given sacred rules to fish or dogs, but to men and women. However, our sacredness has been defiled because we have broken the law.

If someone believes he is good, let him test his goodness. One only has to look at the Ten Commandments to discover how good he is in reality. "Do not lie," he will find written in eternal ink. *I have lied*, he thinks to himself and finds he is a liar. "Do not steal," she finds written. *But I have stolen*, she humbly remembers and finds she is a thief. *I have not committed adultery*, he flatters himself in thinking. But Jesus states that "if you look at woman with lust you commit adultery" (Matt. 5:27-28). Here, we might be frustrated and think God mean to impose such a high standard. In such frustration, we only reveal more of our evil. We know we fall short of perfection, of goodness, and of God. For to lust is to deny the holy worth of an image-bearer. It is to vandalize the painting of God — to desecrate the sacred. After truly examining ourselves, we find quite a bad specimen compared to the standard of good set down by God. We find ourselves not awesome, but appalling.

It is interesting to see that the law only *reveals* that we are bad; it does not make us bad. A law forbidding shoplifting does not make a thief shoplift any more than a command to be kind will make a heart gentle. Humans will act according to their nature. The law only reveals how bad our nature truly is. Because we are sinners, we sin. The fact that we lust does not reveal how good we may be on days we do not lust; it reveals how bad our nature is that we would even desire to lust in the first place. The fact that we must constantly suppress the spring of evil gushing from our souls is ironclad evidence of our depravity. It is our evil nature that desires what is evil. It is the law that shows just how evil our nature truly has become through the fall (Rom 7:7-8). We are wholly broken.

Despite a conscience that bears witness to our own depravity, it's more comfortable to imagine that there is still good in people: *just be the best version of yourself that you can be.* We are to be good boys and girls in order to prove that the good in us is greater than the bad. We try to be good to pay for the bad that we have committed. We try to be good enough to appease our conscience — to convince ourselves that our good deeds will ultimately outweigh the bad. But, just as one plop of cow poop ruins the cookie dough, there is no recovering our souls from the stain of 'badness' with our own acts of imagined 'goodness'.

Imagine a thief who steals a loaf of bread from the market. Once he has chosen to take something that belongs to another, he has traded his honor and honesty for injustice and deceit. There is nothing he can do to right the wrong. He can certainly pay back the lost revenue. A loaf of bread has a set monetary value. But the thief has taken something more than just bread. He has taken away a piece of the shopkeeper's dignity, making the shopkeeper look foolish and abusing the shopkeeper's trust in his character.

The thief might return to the market to plead for forgiveness or even offer to repay the shopkeeper several times more than the value of a loaf of bread in an effort to make things right. But there is no monetary value affixed to dignity. The thief cannot really right the wrong through his own efforts. It is the shopkeeper who must forgive the thief in order to make peace.

With any offense, the price necessary to restore justice and honor depends upon the severity and victim of the crime. Stealing a loaf of bread from a supermarket is one matter; stealing the only loaf of bread from a blind and crippled beggar is quite another. If Hitler had exterminated millions of rabbits it would

have been one evil. Exterminating millions of sacred human beings is quite another. Our evil deeds have an equal cost.

So, what is our cost for breaking God's law? How can humans repay God? Can we work to repay our debts? Let me ask
you this. If you dishonor your mother by slandering her name
can you repay her? Can you give her a certain amount of money that will make restitution for the honor that you have taken?
Even giving her a million dollars would not be enough to right
your wrong. When someone breaks the covenant of marriage,
is there any amount of money that the adulterer can pay to settle the evil debt? No. Is there any number of apologies that can
instantly restore trust in the relationship? No. There are wrong
deeds humans commit against one another that cannot be repaid
with money or any other effort to make up for the mistake. Only
true forgiveness can bring restoration.

If human relationships cannot be mended with our own
efforts, how much more our relationship with Holy God? For
who can dishonor God and repay (Ps. 49:7-8)? When we break
God's law, we break that which is eternally good. We offend the
eternal honor of God. Whenever we sin, we defile a beauty too
pure to behold. When we sin, we dishonor a name too pure to
speak. When we try to repay God with our good deeds, we bring
Monopoly™ money and try to deposit it in the bank. The curren-
cy is no good. We are poor beggars with nothing to appease our
King.

The book of Galatians was written primarily to dismiss
the notion that we can repay God for breaking the law by trying
harder to keep the law. Once we have broken it, as we all have, we
are under the penalty of the law. In Galatians 3:10, Paul warns everyone who thinks that they are good, or 'righteous,' by keeping
the law. He says, "For all who rely on works of the law are under
a curse; for it is written, 'Cursed be everyone who does not abide
by all things written in the Book of the Law, and do them.'" In

breaking even one part of the law, we are responsible for breaking all of it (James 2:10). A person does not need to smash an entire mirror for its perfection to be shattered. One tap to the corner will cause a crack to spider web until the entire mirror is ruined. We are under the curse of sin for breaking the eternal law of God, and the just penalty is death. Trying to put the broken mirror back together will only cause us to ruin it more.

Due to the heinousness of our sin, the Bible unapologetically declares our shocking identity: children of wrath, (Eph. 2:3) dead in our trespasses and sins (Eph. 2:1), enemies of God (Rom. 5:10). We are alienated from God and "hostile in mind, doing evil deeds" (Col. 1:21). We suppress the truth through our unrighteousness and bury any hope of forgiveness under our false pretenses of self-righteousness (Rom. 1:18-21). We sin because it is our very nature. We sin because we are unholy from birth. We are born in sin, David states in Psalm 51. We are born iniquitous traitors set against God. The camp of God's enemy was our nursery, and we hum along with the melodies of God's enemies. We are not good.

Sin has gripped our entire being, thought, will, and emotions, and set us against the purity of God. We have become unlovely and unworthy of love. We have all become corrupt. No amount of work can make us good before God because the law that we are trying to keep constantly reveals how sinful we are (Rom. 3:9-20).

We are poor kids enslaved to sin. Our every intention is corrupt, and our 'good deeds' are as pleasing as ruined rags. We work for sin, and we are paid a wage of death. We have been infected from our conception with a virus which has snuffed out the light of our souls and blinded us from seeing our own condition. We imagine ourselves to be righteous, good enough. But even while we pat ourselves on the back, shame and regret for our unpaid sin convict us again as enemies of God. There is no possible escape from the bondage of sin; there is only hope of rescue.

Unless rescued, we will ultimately feel the weight of our identity as children of wrath in a place called Hell. Hell was originally created for Satan and demons, but now it is for all of God's enemies. Since, like Satan and demons, humanity has fallen and become the enemy of God, those who do not repent and believe in Jesus Christ will experience the wrath of God poured out.

Before payment can be made on our behalf, we must feel the weight of our poverty. We must accept our inability to pay for our own crimes. Those who are well have no need of a doctor (Luke 5:31). The beginning of our rescue is acknowledging our chains. Paul preached openly that he was a sinner, and that message serves as the foundation of his hope and ours:

> The saying is trustworthy and deserving of full acceptance that Christ Jesus came into the world to save sinners, of whom I am the foremost. But I received mercy for this reason, that in me, as the foremost, Jesus Christ might display his perfect patience as an example to those who were to believe in him for eternal life. (1 Timothy 1:15-16)

Own the fact that you are poor before God and can give him nothing — it is the hope of your rich inheritance. Acknowledge that you are weak — it is the hope for your strength in Christ. Call out for salvation, for everyone who calls upon the name of the Lord will be saved.

# RICH KIDS

Jesus' intention is not to make you the best version of yourself. He isn't interested in making you better at all. He is interested in making you alive. His purpose is to make you a child of God. His mission is to rescue you from your poor condition and to clothe you in riches in the Kingdom of God.

We have seen how we are in no way deserving of becoming children of God. We have seen that we deserve Hell, and God is fully justified to send us there. When someone breaks the law, the penalty set down against them is just. When someone speeds on the highway, the police officer is simply delivering justice when he hands the driver a 'ticket to the circus,' as my grandfather used to say. When someone commits murder, the jury is simply delivering justice when they declare a sentence. To call the jury 'mean' for penalizing the murderer would be misguided. Similarly, God is not being mean by delivering justice to those who break his law. Do we not rejoice when a TV villain is defeated? Don't we find satisfaction in the execution of justice? How much more just, then, is God in defending the purity of his eternal law by punishing its offenders.

The bad news is we all deserve Hell. Here is the good news: God is, as Moses said, "merciful and gracious, slow to anger, and abounding in steadfast love and faithfulness" (Ex. 34:6). We are like convicted murderers, hearts pounding, palms sweating, standing at the gallows waiting for our sentence to be carried out when, suddenly, the judge signs a proclamation and another man is hanged in our place. *What? This has got to be a joke. What kind of mind trick is this?* we would think. The judge informs us that our death sentence has been carried out on another man. If we choose to accept the other man's payment offered for our guilt, we are free to go. The noose is lifted from our neck. The charges against us are dropped. We are declared innocent and our hands are liberated from their shackles. "Who would do this?" we ask. "My only son," the judge whispers in our ears. Our hearts are struck with the mercy revealed, and we fall to the ground in disbelief.

I know it is hard to believe that Jesus Christ, God in skin, would die for his enemies. It is hard to believe that he would even care to send his enemies a greeting card, let alone give his life as a ransom for their own. But the gospel is so much more than the fact that Jesus died for the forgiveness of the sins of all who believe in him. He also offers us a new identity. Freed slaves, we become holy children of God, heirs of the Kingdom of God, clothed in immortal glory.

Kind of sounds like a no-brainer, right? Be a poor kid enslaved to sin which pays wages of death, or be a rich kid by receiving the forgiveness of God and become his child and an heir to his Kingdom (Rom. 6:23; 8:17). The fact that we would even think of despising such a merciful offer only displays the complete evil of our fallen nature.

You may now understand why you find Christians unconcerned about gaining wealth on earth. It might be clearer why you find Christians unimpressed with the glory offered by fame. You may understand why Christians have a spirit of contentment and hope. You may be seeing for the first time that Christians are rich kids. They are not working to become someone; they have been made children of God and are waiting patiently for their inheritance (Heb. 6:12). Christians are not impressed with what the world has to offer because what God offers them in Christ is eternally greater.

Let's be explicitly clear. There are only two types of children according to God: poor kids and rich kids, sinners and saints, children of wrath and children of God. "Whoever believes in the Son has eternal life," John tells us; "Whoever does not obey the Son shall not see life, but the wrath of God remains on him" (John 3:36). If you have not repented and believed in Jesus Christ for the forgiveness of your sins, you are a child of wrath — a poor kid. You only become a child of God — a rich kid — when you receive the forgiveness offered in the blood of Jesus Christ, poured out for the pardon of sins forever. And, according to God's word, you receive a lot more than forgiveness.

When we repent of our sins and believe in the salvation offered in Jesus Christ, our new identity as his children secures our hope for this life and our eternal future. We receive "every spiritual blessing in heavenly places" (Eph. 1:3). *How do I know this is true?* Because every word of God proves to be true. *Why would I want blessings in heaven?* Because heaven's blessings are forever. They are incorruptible, and better than any blessing on earth. *What are those spiritual blessings?* I'm glad you asked.

We are chosen — called by name and picked by God's own choice. "He [Jesus] chose us in him before the foundation of the world" (Eph. 1:4). There is no feeling like feeling desired. Every athlete wants to be picked for the team. All humans want to be desired for friendship and relationship. The longing in our marrow to be desired is satisfied in this reality: Christ has chosen you. Long before we had breath in our lungs, those who believe in Jesus Christ were marked by the affection of God and loved by his choice. We were not worthy, but Christ has not chosen us because of anything we have done. "For by grace you have been saved through faith," Paul declares. "And this is not your own doing; it is the gift of God, not a result of works, so that no one may boast" (Eph. 2:8-9). You are not second best; in Christ you are God's first choice.

We were not only chosen by God's grace, we are also made righteous. We are blameless – made pure, washed clean, made holy. We were chosen so "that we should be holy and blameless before him" (Eph. 1:4). We have not been made *better*. We have been made *new*. We have been raised from death to life. The miracle that happens when someone is "born again," as Jesus said, is that sinners become saints.

"Well, I'm just a sinner saved by grace" is a popular 'Christianese' saying, particularly used to feign humility when praised by others. Though a seemingly harmless phrase, it misses a huge point of the gospel: you have been given a *new* life. You are no longer a 'sinner' in identity, but a saint. When we become Christians, it is as transformative as a pig becoming a man — we have been born of a new race.

Think about the former pig for a moment. His very DNA has been irreversibly altered from animal to human. He may go and lay in the mud, but he will never actually become a pig again. Of course, it is unfit for a man to lay in the mud as if he were a pig, but he is simply not acting according to his new nature as a man. When you've been a pig for your whole life, it is easy to slip back into old habits. But reverting to a pig's ways does not make you a pig. He's not just a 'pig saved from the mud'; he's a new man.

In the same way, saints may sin, but that is only because they are learning the rules of their new nature. 'Saint' (ἅγιος) is a term which actually means 'holy ones' or 'sacred ones.' The term 'holy' means set apart, sacred, or other. Their new nature is in a completely different category. When sinners repent and believe in Jesus Christ, they are made saints. They are made sacred. They are made of entirely new matter (1 Cor. 15:47-49). Sinners are made of the broken material of Adam. Saints are made of the imperishable atoms of Jesus Christ. Because of their new nature, saints now hate rolling in the mud; they have been made new.

Saints are righteous. They have not been made perfect by being good boys and girls but by the power and forgiveness of God. Saints have died and been brought back to life as perfect immortals. Christ has raised the former race to new life, covering the sins of all who believe in him (Heb. 4:10). Jesus justifies all saints so that they are without sin in the sight of God (Rom. 5:1). Saints are no longer under the oppression of guilt and shame. There is no condemnation for those who are in Christ Jesus (Rom. 8:1). Jesus killed their condemnation on the cross and buried it with his body (Rom. 6:7). He raised to immortality, realizing our hope of perfection and giving us rest from our own struggle to be free.

Saints are also children of God. God, "predestined us for adoption to himself as sons through Jesus Christ, according to the purpose of his will, to the praise of his glorious grace" (Eph. 1:5-6). We have been adopted. We have become a part of a family that holds endless riches and perfect love. All those "who [have] believed in His [Jesus'] name, He gave the right to become children of God," John unveils; "Children born not of blood, nor of the desire or will of man, but born of God" (John 1:12-13). We are children of the Most High, a privilege that is given by the grace of God.

Being a child of God is a privilege only extended to humanity through faith in Jesus Christ. We have seen that our good works — even those done in Jesus' name — or our own efforts to fix ourselves will not qualify us for heaven. We cannot climb into God's family any other way than walking through the door of Jesus Christ (John 10:9). Jesus says that he needs to "know" us if we are to be granted admission (Matt. 7:23). He must know us as a brother knows a sister and as a man knows his wife. He must know us intimately through relationship. If you want to go to Jesus' house, you have to know Jesus. The Father doesn't allow just anyone into his home, but he certainly lets his children enter (Matt. 25:34).

Adoption is a permanent position which cannot be withdrawn. When God chooses you, he chooses you forever. When you become a child of God through adoption, you are a son forever.

In first century culture, if the master of the house wanted to make one of his slaves a son, he offered him adoption. The slave had a choice to accept or reject the offer. If he chose to accept, paperwork was filed, and once the slave and the master signed the legal adoption papers, that slave was a son forever.

The slave-become-son now shared all the rights and privileges as the biological son. 'Sonship' is an important idea to highlight, here. Historically, kingdoms and inheritances of money and property usually passed to the oldest male in the family. Calling us 'sons,' then, is not a diss on daughters; it merely reveals that men and women who are in Christ are legally given the keys to the kingdom under the rule of Christ. We are adopted as children of God, Paul says in Romans 8:17: "and if children, then heirs—heirs of God and fellow heirs with Christ, provided we suffer with him in order that we may also be glorified with him." This great mercy lavished upon us was done to demonstrate the glorious grace of God in Christ.

Like modern adoptions, our adoption was not free. First, we had to be redeemed – bought back from slavery (Rom. 7:14). Paul speaking to the church in Galatia says, "Christ redeemed us from the curse of the law by becoming a curse for us—for it is written, 'Cursed is everyone who is hanged on a tree'" (Gal. 3:13). Salvation is a benefit we experience for free. But, salvation was expensive; it cost the blood of Christ. Paul clarifies the point:

> In him we have redemption through his blood, the forgiveness of our trespasses, according to the riches of his grace, which he lavished upon us, in all wisdom and insight making known to us the mystery of his will, according to his purpose, which he set forth in Christ as a plan for the fullness of time, to unite all things in him, things in heaven and things on earth. (Ephesians 1:7-10)

Our redemption is only a part of the plan of God to redeem all things through Jesus Christ. Jesus has bought back the cosmos with his blood. He has destroyed evil so he can remake Eden more glorious than ever. He has redeemed all things so that we might praise the glory of his grace and power forever and ever when he makes the cosmos perfect again.

We are redeemed in Christ, but we are also rich in Christ. We have become co-heirs with Christ of the great inheritance of the Kingdom of Heaven. You have heard of the prosperity gospel — the idea that if you believe in Jesus, he will make you rich. I would like to propose to you that the gospel is, in itself, prosperity. In Jesus Christ, we are made rich through our heavenly inheritance. The riches of earth, which perish, are nothing compared to the riches of the Kingdom of God, which last forever.

True Christians are not content in the riches of earth; they long for the riches that are theirs in heaven. "In him [Christ]," Paul says, "we have obtained an inheritance, having been predestined according to the purpose of him who works all things according to the counsel of his will" (Eph. 1:11). In Christ, our inheritance is presently obtained; we do not need to work for it. In Christ, God is pleased to share the riches of his Kingdom with his adopted sons. We are rich kids!

Our inheritance is also sealed. We are sealed by the Holy Spirit of God (John 3:33; Acts 10:44, 47). When we become a child of God we receive the seal of God in the person of the Holy Spirit:

> In him you also, when you heard the word of truth, the gospel of your salvation, and believed in him, were sealed with the promised Holy Spirit, who is the guarantee of our inheritance until we acquire possession of it, to the praise of his glory (Ephesians 1:13-14).

Throughout history, when a king made an edict, he affixed his seal to the document, authenticating it and declaring that it was given by his authority. When we are saved, the genuine mark placed on those who believe in Jesus Christ is the Holy

Spirit. The Holy Spirit, who convicts of sin and protects and preserves Christians from sin, is the certificate of authenticity that the individual knows Christ by faith (Eph. 4:30; 2 Cor. 1:22; 1 Peter 1:5; Rev. 7:2-3). If someone is concerned about whether or not they are saved, they need only ask one question: have I received the Spirit of God? In Galatians 5:16-26, Paul describes how we can examine our lives and search our hearts to see if we hold the seal of God – The Holy Spirit, full of love, joy, peace, patience, kindness, gentleness, goodness, and self-control.

Rest in the fact that you are a child of God. Cling to the hope of your inheritance in him. If you have not repented from sin and become a child of God, simply turn to God and be made new. "Turn to me and be saved, all the ends of the earth! For I am God, and there is no other" (Is. 45:22). In our rest, let us glorify God, for his mercy is amazing!

God in His riches reached down to us — dirty paupers. First, he set his affection upon us. So many people have failed to set their true affection upon us, but Christ has. Then, he said we are forgiven. None has purposed to take the punishment that we deserved, but Christ has. Finally, he adopted us and made us his sons. Who has said they will give to us their wealth? God has.

Now that we rest in the Master's house and are called by His Name, clothed in Royal splendor, and given a place in the Kingdom, shall we praise our own name? Shall we give glory to ourselves when we have done nothing to reach our esteemed position? No, all the glory is given to God, for not only has he died for us, he has also made us Royals. He has not only bought us back, but he has also given us riches beyond measure. He has satisfied the longing in our souls for wealth and belonging, which we could never satisfy on our own.

God's glory — his intensity, his honor, his majesty, his grace, his mercy, his love — never wanes. Even now, the cosmos loses its glory. The sun begins to tire, losing the perfection with which it was made. But we shall never lose the glory and perfection we have been given. The Son forever shines on us, giving perfect life.

In Christ, we are sealed with the Royal Seal; the decree is set in Royal Ink. No more must we question if we are loved, for we are loved eternally. No more must we strive to please others, for God is pleased with us in Christ. We must not work for an inheritance, for the Kingdom shall be given to us. We share in the inheritance as one of the brothers. We are rich kids.

# MEANING

*When a person can't find a deep sense of meaning, they distract themselves with pleasure.*

**VIKTOR FRANKL**

*God's purpose for my life was that I have a passion for God's glory and that I have a passion for my joy in that glory, and that these two are one passion.*

**JONATHAN EDWARDS**

*If the whole universe has no meaning, we should never have found out that it has no meaning: just as, if there were no light in the universe and therefore no creatures with eyes, we should never know it was dark. Dark would be without meaning.*

**C.S. LEWIS**

*Without God, life has no purpose, and without purpose, life has no meaning. Without meaning, life has no significance or hope. The ultimate goal of the universe is to show the glory of God.*

**RICK WARREN**

*Since barbarism has its pleasures it naturally has its apologists.*

**GEORGE SANTAYANA**

*I've been sleeping in for days,*
*'Cause when I am awake,*
*I will have to face my life.*

**NEVERTHELESS**

# MEANING
## GLORY

## GAMES

Games are undercover tutors of the meaning of life. Imagine you show up late for a sporting event. What's the first thing you ask your friends: What is the score? The question is the same whether you're watching a quidditch match or a football game. It may seem like mindless curiosity, but this question unmasks a hidden longing in the desire of our soul – the desire to win. We enjoy watching games because in the end, there are winners. In all sport, there is something to gain and something to lose.

We watch the same game over and over again, season after season, year after year because — while the game is the same — it is always new. There are always new players, new coaches, and new opportunities to win glory. Players play for glory — a trophy, money, fame — and fans cheer their teams on that they might share in that glory.

While competitors play for glory in the form of medals or attention, the true meaning of sport is not rooted in material glory. For example, if a player cheats in order to win, no one applauds. "What a loser," both fans and rivals say. If the meaning of sport was only about victory and ensuing reward, we wouldn't care how the athletes achieved the end — cheating would be perfectly acceptable. But, 'winning' is comprised of more refined substance than trophies, medals, and fame.

On August 16th, 2016, at the Olympic Games in Rio De Janeiro, Abbey D'Agostino of the USA and Nikki Hamblin of New Zealand were competing in the second heat of the women's 5,000 meters. After a nasty fall, both found themselves lying on the track with no hope of victory. Then something remarkable happened. Having risen to finish the race, D'Agostino stopped, went back, and helped Hamblin to her feet. When D'Agostino later stumbled again due to injury, Hamblin helped D'Agostino to hers. Both finished the race. Both crossed the finish line.

D'Agostino crossed the finish line in last place with a time of 17:10.02 and Hamblin next-to-last with a time of 16:43.61. But, their race times are not remembered. They were eclipsed in an instant by what happened next. After crossing the finish line both women hugged in a beautiful tear-filled embrace. "I am so grateful to Abbey for helping me," Hamblin told a reporter. "That girl [D'Agostino] was the Olympic spirit right there. I am so impressed and inspired by that." The whole world had a lump in its throat.

A beautiful victory unfolded, yet neither of those women won a medal. The Olympic Committee allowed both women to run in the finals, but injured D'Agostino watched from the stands — the whole world knowing her name. Both received the Rio 2016 Fair Play Award presented by the International Fair Play

Committee. Apparently, the Olympic spirit isn't about winning gold medals. It is about winning something greater.

Far more than winning the glory of an Olympic medal, D'Agostino and Hamblin won the respect of billions of people worldwide and honor for their name that cannot be wiped away. That moment was beautiful and praiseworthy because the end goal of the game of life — the meaning of humanity — is to receive glory that does not fade and crowns that do not perish. Life has a purpose, and this purpose gives life its meaning. We live for one ultimate end: Glory. We play for glory only because we live for it.

## MEANING? WHAT MEANING?

Consider, for a moment, the effect that purpose has on our behavior. Your professor enters class, drops a textbook on the desk, and says, "this is our book. I want you to read it. But, it has nothing to do with our class work, and I promise never to test you on it." Most of the students in the class will not bother to read the book. What's the point? Or, maybe your boss tells you to paint as many window shutters as you can in an hour. If she promises you ten dollars per shutter, your efforts may be slightly increased than if she promises you ten dollars per hour. Our end goal affects our sense of purpose.

The same is true in our worldview. If we accept the lie that there was no meaning to the beginning of our lives, and there will be no meaning to the end of our lives, then what hope do we have in the living of our lives? The answer is none. No purpose. No glory. Only the logical despair that our trivial pursuits mean nothing now because they will mean nothing in the end. If history is not moving to a purposeful conclusion then there is not an atom of meaning in time and space. If no one is keeping score, if no honor can be won, why play? No end goal, no purpose.

Those who hold a naturalistic, or non-supernatural, belief system try to overcome the problem of meaning by suggesting it can be found in natural pleasures. "Meaning is what we make it," or "I find meaning in the here and now... my family, friends, work, and fun." Sadly, relying on the here and now for meaning leads to a false sense of purpose. Meaning cannot even be defined with no eternal point of reference. Friends and family are a random clump of atoms if they were not created with intention. Work and fun are just distractions from the reality of our own random and inconsequential existence.

A person cannot become more or less honorable if ultimate and lasting honor is not a prize. A competitor cannot move closer to winning a trophy if there is no trophy to win. If there is no glory to gain at the end of life, there is no purpose in the living of life. We are all just frantically reading the professor's textbook and trying to suppress the fact that it won't mean anything in the end.

Time after time, naturalistic thinkers have acknowledged the futility of their pursuits for meaning within the natural world. They find the object of their own definition of meaning to be meaningless. In their unsatisfied chase, they teach us that meaning rests on a higher peak.

Jack Higgens, the author of several popular novels including *The Eagle has Landed*, was once asked what he wished he had been told as a boy. His answer was remarkable. He replied, "That when you get to the top, there's nothing there." *What do you mean Jack? That you climbed to the summit of success and it was empty of meaning and joy?* That is exactly what he was saying. And, he is not alone in his discovery.

At the 2016 Golden Globe Awards, the comedic legend Jim Carrey, while presenting the nominees for Best Motion Picture Comedy, delivered an existential seminar smothered in sarcasm. After being introduced as, "Two-time Golden Globe winner Jim Carrey," he joked about someday becoming the satisfied "*Three-time* Golden Globe winner Jim Carrey."

"Because," he jabbed satirically, "Then it would finally be enough. It would finally be true...And I could stop this terrible search...for what I know ultimately won't fulfill me." In an attempt to bring purpose back to the moment, he joked, "But these are important, these awards." Then, after describing the theoretical destruction of our solar system and poking fun at the meaninglessness of human achievement, Carrey ended with, "But, from our perspective, this [award] is huge."

A comedic legend unsatisfied with his accomplishments and searching for meaning? That is a tragedy. A tragedy played out in the life of another great comedic hero – Robin Williams. A life of humor and joy ended in suicide. Glory not found; only despair.

We could list many individuals who, having achieved the pinnacle of success in life, found no lasting meaning in their accomplishments and committed suicide. It is with great reverence that we must approach this subject because death and depression are very serious topics. We must acknowledge even more seriously that a worldview devoid of an end purpose robs individuals of any orientation to identity, meaning, purpose, and ultimately hope in life. Suicide is only a fruit plucked from the tree of a naturalistic worldview. Not everyone eats the fruit, but it dangles from its branches nevertheless.

When we test a theory repeatedly and it proves to be false, we should be prepared to admit that the theory is wrong. But generation after generation, age after age, we find men and women reaching the pinnacle of human achievement and still failing to find meaning. It is like we have searched our whole lives for hidden treasure only to unearth the chest, pry open its lid, and find nothing but air. Our pursuit for pleasure is always letting us down.

Insanity, it is said, is repeating the same action and expecting different results. Our greatest insanity as the human race is not that we have found the same empty treasure chest that has been found by generations before. The insanity is that we bury it and dig it up again, hoping somehow, someway, that the treasure of meaning which we search for continuously, will magically appear. We think that a new approach to the same end will yield different results. Take comfort in the fact that our disappointment is not new.

Solomon, King of Israel, known for his wealth, his wisdom, and his writings wrote an entire book about his experimental testing of the meaning of life. "Vanity of vanities! All is vanity," or a 'vapor,' he declares in the opening chapter of Ecclesiastes. The problem with answers that are 'blowin' in the wind,' Solomon would conclude, is that they blow away.

In Ecclesiastes, Solomon catalogues all of the vain life goals in which he attempted to find meaning. He observed the cyclical vanity of nature. The sun rises, sets, and rises again. The wind blows and circles the earth, only to return to where it first raged. Streams run to the sea and never fill it up. Instead, it fills only to empty again. The eye sees and is never satisfied. The ear hears but listens for more and never tires of hearing. What has been done before will be done again. He concludes there is nothing new under the sun (Eccles. 1:5-9).

He also studied the empty pursuit of wisdom and knowledge as ends in themselves. "And I applied my heart to know wisdom," he writes, "and to know madness and folly. I perceived that this also is but a striving after wind. For in much wisdom is much vexation, and he who increases knowledge increases sorrow" (Eccles. 1:17-18). The end of wisdom and knowledge is not joy, but sadness, he states — not freedom from sorrow, but greater knowledge of it.

Solomon then examined the meaning of pleasures, possessions, and accomplishments. He had drunk wine, gathered a huge harem of women, and obtained servants. He built houses, vineyards, gardens, parks and orchards. He gathered gold and silver, livestock and immense wealth so that he was wealthier than all the kings of the earth (2 Chron. 9:22; 1 Kings 10:14-22). He had tasted every pleasure known to mankind in abundance. Instead of saying that he was satisfied, he declared the emptiness of all these treasures:

> And whatever my eyes desired I did not keep from them. I kept my heart from no pleasure, for my heart found pleasure in all my toil, and this my reward for all my toil. Then I considered all that my hands had done and the toil I had expended in doing it, and behold, all was vanity and a striving after wind, and there was nothing to be gained under the sun. (Ecclesiastes 2:10-11)

The very wisdom through which Solomon was viewing the world became, in his eyes, only vanity. In his wisdom, he perceived that despite his wisdom, he could not escape the same end destined for the fool:

> Then I said in my heart, "What happens to the fool will happen to me also. Why then have I been so very wise?" And I said in my heart that this also is vanity. For of the wise as of the fool there is no enduring remembrance, seeing that in the days to come all will have been long forgotten. How the wise dies just like the fool! So I hated life, because what is done under the sun was grievous to me, for all is vanity and a striving after wind. (Ecclesiastes 2:15-17)

He goes on and on in his discovery of vanities. He despised the vanity of work. "I hated all my toil in which I toil under the sun, seeing that I must leave it to the man who will come after me, and who knows whether he will be wise or a fool?" (Eccles. 2:18-19). Solomon was coming to grips with the fact that all he had acquired he would have to leave to someone who did not work for it. Naturally, it led to despair. And, in that despair, he exposed the vanity of all mortal life:

> For what happens to the children of man and what happens to the beasts is the same; as one dies, so dies the other. They all have the same breath, and man has no advantage over the beasts, for all is vanity. All go to one place. All are from the dust, and to dust all return. (Ecclesiastes 3:19-20)

Solomon had pursued every pleasurable end he could possibly think of — sex, power, knowledge, fame, wealth — and found that all of them were empty of satisfaction. Solomon learned that pleasure for pleasure's sake was as a match burning in passionate flame only for a moment and then extinguished forever – meaningless.

It is not that there is *no* pleasure or glory in the ends that we may pursue. It is that these ends leave us longing for *greater* pleasure and glory. Whatever glorious pleasure we imagine will be found in the natural world will leave us wanting more.

Hedonism is the idea that pleasure alone is our highest aim. This points us in the right direction — we were, in fact, created to pursue pleasure. But, time after time, the simple pursuit of pleasure leaves us longing for more because true pleasure is found in a higher end.

Our pride convinces us that there is no higher purpose than seeking our own pleasure for our own sake. And, when we cannot find satisfaction in that endeavor, we are driven to despair. We are like actors pouting on a stage because, after choosing to improvise our own story rather than following the master script, no one applauded our selfishness. We cannot understand that in choosing to exalt ourselves, we are belittled. Here, humility finally has a chance to whisper in our ear true delight: there is One greater than ourselves and a joy greater than we now know. It is when we are down that we learn to look up.

Finally, we begin to listen to the eternal longing of our souls for a greater glory. We long for a sweeter sugar. The honey that we have indulged in is no longer sweet to our taste. The words spoken by Christians — 'eternal rewards,' 'eternal glory,' and 'everlasting life' — begin to sound lovely. Here, the truth dawns on us: we have been settling for less when more has been offered.

God desires our pleasure. He desires our ultimate happiness (John 15:11, 17:13). We have mistakenly believed that we would be happy apart from God and the joy he offers. As C.S. Lewis keenly observed:

> It would seem that Our Lord finds our desires not too strong, but too weak. We are half-hearted creatures, fooling about with drink and sex and ambition when infinite joy is offered us, like an ignorant child who wants to go on making mud pies in a slum because he cannot imagine what is meant by the offer of a holiday at the sea. We are far too easily pleased.

Once we are willing to set down the glory offered on earth, we have room in our hands to reach for the glory offered in heaven. Hope fills our souls again, and our hunt for true treasure begins. Eternity knows no limit to pleasure, and it is wise to look there.

# GLORY

Solomon ends Ecclesiastes with a redeeming statement of human purpose, finally naming the highest peak of pleasure – God. "The end of the matter; all has been heard." He closes, "Fear God and keep his commandments, for this is the whole duty of man. For God will bring every deed into judgment, with every secret thing, whether good or evil" (Eccles. 12:13-14). After a search for self-centered meaning, Solomon discovers that our true meaning is to glorify — praise, honor, ascribe greatest worth to — God.

Our fallen nature wants to immediately dismiss this thought as desperately childish. Surely something we can do or achieve can produce lasting meaning and eternal glory for ourselves. To that end, we pursue earthly pleasure because we believe it will bring us joy. And it does, but only a sort of vaporous joy that vanishes quickly. We try indulging in the pleasure once more only to find it dissolve like a vanishing snow on a spring morning. Eventually, we become tired with that pleasure altogether and look for another until it produces the same undesirable effect. So, we come to the rational end of the search. We despair that there is no pleasure to be found in life. In finding our life, we have lost it. We have worked for pleasure, but it proved to be a stingy master. We labored for joy and became poor, joyless shadows.

Having searched under every rock and come up empty, our souls are still left aching for eternal glory. We have innate expectations of eternal pleasure and consuming joy (Eccles. 3:11) — we certainly know when they are missing. From where have those expectations sprung? We have not placed them in our own souls. Rather, in his goodness, our Maker has created a longing within us so strong that only he can satisfy, as the highest glory and greatest imaginable joy.

God is glory. He is immortal. He dwells in unapproachable light. He is power (1 Timothy 6:16). All who see God cry,
"Glory!" (Ps. 29:9). John sees a vision of God and falls down as
though dead (Rev. 1:17). Ezekiel sees a manifestation of the glory of God and falls to his face (Ez. 1). Moses and the writer of
Hebrews liken God's glory to a consuming fire (Heb. 12:29; Ex.
24:27). Jesus' face "shone like the sun" at his transfiguration and
his clothes became "white as light" (Matt. 17:2). Isaiah sees the
glory of The LORD and records his encounter:

> In the year that King Uzziah died I saw the Lord
> sitting upon a throne, high and lifted up; and the
> train of his robe filled the temple. Above him
> stood the seraphim. Each had six wings: with two
> he covered his face, and with two he covered his
> feet, and with two he flew. And one called to an-
> other and said:
>
> "Holy, holy, holy is the LORD of hosts;
>
> The whole earth is full of his glory!"
>
> And the foundations of the thresholds shook at
> the voice of him who called, and the house was
> filled with smoke. And I said: "Woe is me! For
> I am lost; for I am a man of unclean lips, and I
> dwell in the midst of a people of unclean lips; for
> my eyes have seen the King, the LORD of hosts!"
> (Isaiah 6:1-6)

The glory of God makes the foundations of the cosmos
shake. It was from the contents of God's own glory that all other
glory was made. "For from Him and through Him and to Him
are all things," Paul says; "To Him be the glory forever! Amen"
(Rom. 11:36). His beauty is his glory. His love is his glory. His ho-

liness is his glory. He is excellent — glorious — from everlasting to everlasting (Phil. 4:20).

Selfish pleasure is finite. It ends. God's glory is infinite. It will never end. Whenever we make seeking God's glory our end, we align our highest aim with the highest glory. Seeking the glory of God is to seek our joy, for in glorifying God we bring delight to ourselves. The Bible overflows with endorsement for the pleasure found in God:

> You make known to me the path of life; in your presence there is fullness of joy; at your right hand are pleasures forevermore. (Psalm 16:11)

> I will rejoice and be glad in your lovingkindness, Because you have seen my affliction; you have known the troubles of my soul. (Psalm 31:7)

> They feast on the abundance of your house, and you give them drink from the river of your delights. (Psalm 36:8)

> How blessed is the one whom you choose and bring near to you to dwell in your courts. We will be satisfied with the goodness of your house, your holy temple. (Psalm 65:4)

> Will you not yourself revive us again, that your people may rejoice in you? (Psalm 85:6)

> Satisfy us in the morning with your steadfast love that we may rejoice and be glad all our days. (Psalm 90:14)

> Why do you spend your money for that which is not bread, and your labor for that which does not

satisfy? Listen diligently to me, and eat what is good, and delight yourselves in rich food. (Isaiah 55:2)

I will feast the soul of the priests with abundance, and my people shall be satisfied with my goodness, declares the LORD. (Jeremiah 31:14)

Joy is found in God. Joy is found in community with others who believe in the true God and His Son Jesus Christ because God is found in them. When someone believes in Jesus Christ, they receive joy because they receive God – the substance of eternal joy. They receive God in their body through the person of the Holy Spirit. Peter spoke of this truth thousands of years ago, saying "Repent and be baptized every one of you in the name of Jesus Christ for the forgiveness of your sins, and you will receive the gift of the Holy Spirit" (Acts 2:38). Eternal joy takes up residence in the souls of all who trust in Jesus for salvation (1 Cor. 6:19-20).

The source of a believer's eternal joy is God's glory. Think about the connection between emotions of joy and glory. When we get a promotion, build a new house, marry our lover, receive a compliment, or get an "A," our personal glory increases, and we are happy. Because glory increases, our joy increases. Whenever our glory decreases — losing a game, making a mistake, failing a test — we experience sadness. When our glory chamber seems completely empty, we feel depression – a deep and unending sadness.

Since glory controls our joy, the absence or presence of glory will increase or decrease our joy. For believers of Jesus, the Holy Spirit — Glory itself — has manifested himself in their body, so we can experience true and lasting satisfaction. We are bonded to the glory of God on a level beyond scientific observation. The presence of God's eternal glory is forever satisfying the longing for pleasure in the soul of a Christian.

*Wait, so you don't ever have a bad day or get sad?* When Christians talk about their lasting joy, it can be tempting to doubt their claims. It's true that even believers who know the glory of God in an intimate way still experience the struggles of life. The difference is that they don't have to try desperately to fill their glory tanks with their own power. They have an eternal supply of God's glory in the Holy Spirit. They feel fear, but the very present glory of God comforts them. They feel stress, but the glory of God's love assures them that he will provide perfectly for their needs. They experience sorrow, but believers have hope because God's glory has defeated death. Their joy never ceases because God's glory within them never changes.

The natural overflow of holding such abundant joy is praise. Our chief end is to glorify God and to enjoy him forever. The two are one. In glorifying God, we find our highest joy. John Piper coined the term 'Christian Hedonism' to describe the source of the joy of Christians. Christians are most satisfied — find the most pleasure — when they glorify God. This is the reason we were created – to praise God. Praise for ourselves is not fitting when we know God through the supernatural presence of the Holy Spirit. There is a far greater glory and power present.

Everything we do has the potential to honor God. Paul said in 1 Corinthians 10:31 "So, whether you eat or drink, or whatever you do, do all to the glory of God." Later in Colossians 3:23-24, he says, "Whatever you do, work heartily, as for the Lord and not for men knowing that from the Lord you will receive the inheritance as your reward. You are serving the Lord Jesus Christ." Meaning is found in this eternal end: that we live to honor God.

Consider a final example of the difference between earthly and eternal glory. Our first character is a famous YouTube personality. She has lots of followers, endorsement deals, and money. She rules a mini-universe and basks in the momentary glory that society, with its short attention span, gives her. Despite her earthly glory, she thinks, *In the end, what have I gained? Even if I manage to stay relevant in this life, when I die, I can't take my money, videos, or followers with me.* She will despair at the thought. She sees that her glory will fade into endless shadow. Without the possibility of having glory forever, she has no joy or meaning now.

Our second character manages a local restaurant. Every moment, she thanks God for her job and the strength to work. She is always glorifying God – because the glory of God dwells in her body in the Spirit. She works hard day in and day out because she works to honor her Maker. Her life has meaning because she works for an end outside of herself. She works for the highest end – the glory of God. So, she feels that even her most nominal tasks, like filling salt and pepper shakers or clearing tables, are eternally valuable because she works for eternal rewards. She has little money, but she has joy and meaning. No one looks to her for social trends or pays her to travel, but she has a joy that is forever – she works for glory that is eternal.

"Everything happens for a reason" has become a cliché – but, it is true. Every single event in human history is working for the singular purpose of glorifying God. "The LORD has made everything for its purpose," Solomon says; "even the wicked for the day of trouble" (Prov. 16:4). All of world history is converging to one fixed point. Every one of us is speeding toward glory: we all are on a collision course with Christ (Rom.14:11; Rev. 20:11-12). It is this end which gives meaning to everything we do.

All of life has meaning because it has a purpose: the glory of God. It does not matter whether we believe that this is the purpose of life. A child on a cruise ship charted for Antigua may believe he is destined for the moon, but he will ultimately arrive in Antigua either way. Regardless of our belief, the course of our lives is set to meet the glory of God. Here is where Solomon finally ended his search for meaning – at the End. He had encouraged all people to fear God and keep his commands, "For God will bring every deed into judgement, with every secret thing, whether good or evil" (Eccles. 12:14). Any meaning today — until that final day — is rooted in the fact that God is keeping score and is going to reward or punish based on our performance.

All throughout the Bible, the meaning of life is rooted in the fact that as we glorify God, we are rewarded.

> If your enemy is hungry, give him bread to eat, and if he is thirsty, give him water to drink, for you will heap burning coals on his head, and the LORD will reward you. (Proverbs 25:21-22)

> I, the LORD, search the heart, I test the mind, Even to give to each man according to his ways, according to the results of his deeds. (Jeremiah 17:10)

> But when you give to the needy, do not let your left hand know what your right hand is doing, so that your giving may be in secret. And your Father who sees in secret will reward you. (Matthew 6:3-4)

> But when you pray, go into your room and shut the door and pray to your Father who is in secret. And your Father who sees in secret will reward you. (Matthew 6:6)

> His master said to him, "Well done, good and faithful servant. You have been faithful over a lit-

tle; I will set you over much. Enter into the joy of your master." (Matthew 25:21)

Then the King will say to those on His right, "Come, you who are blessed by my Father, inherit the kingdom prepared for you from the foundation of the world." (Matthew 25:34)

Nothing in all creation is hidden from God's sight; everything is uncovered and exposed before the eyes of Him to whom we must give account. (Hebrews 4:13)

I press on toward the goal to win the prize for which God has called me heavenward in Christ Jesus. (Philippians 3:14)

To the one who is victorious, I will grant the right to sit with Me on My throne, just as I overcame and sat down with My Father on His throne. (Revelation 3:21)

Jesus himself modeled a perfect life of meaning. He spent all of his energy glorifying God by doing the Father's will (Luke 22:42). Jesus lived a life of purpose because he did not live for his own glory. Jesus, God himself, modeled for all humanity that true meaning is glorifying God. "Now My soul is troubled, and what shall I say?" Jesus cried, "'Father, save Me from this hour?' No, it is for this purpose that I have come to this hour. Father, glorify Your name!" Then a voice came from heaven: "I have glorified it, and I will glorify it again" (John 12:27-28). Every moment of Jesus' life was lived for the singular eternal purpose of glorifying God's name.

A wasted life is a life lived for empty glory. We have been created to pursue the highest glory: God's glory. Every other pursuit of glory is meaningless in the end. The writer of Hebrews encourages us to set our eyes on the prize of the glory of God and the joy that fills our lives when we pursue that end:

> Therefore, since we are surrounded by so great a cloud of witnesses, let us also lay aside every weight, and sin which clings so closely, and let us run with endurance the race that is set before us, looking to Jesus, the founder and perfecter of our faith, who for the joy that was set before him endured the cross, despising the shame, and is seated at the right hand of the throne of God. (Hebrews 12: 1-2)

Christ pursued the highest glory because he knew where the highest glory rests. He did not spend his life pursuing fame. He knew that fame is sentenced to this life. He did not spend his life pursuing riches. He knew that riches mold and melt. He did not create his own meaning. He knew that false meaning dies with its orator. He exalted God in his life. He sought the highest meaning and the highest joy: the glory of God.

How do we glorify God? We simply thank him. We honor him always. "The one who offers thanksgiving as his sacrifice glorifies me," (Ps. 50:23) Scripture teaches. All things are God's – including us. Every mountain and molecule is God's. Every breath and every fiber of our being is God's (Ps. 100:3). It is only fitting that we honor God.

We do not have to go to college or change careers to glorify God. We only have to change our aim. Every morning that you rise and thank God for your breath you glorify Him. Every moment that you are on the clock, working as if for God, you glorify Him. Every time you eat a delicious steak and you praise God for beef you glorify Him. Every nominal task of your day that you use to glorify God is eternally significant.

If you have no joy, it could be that you have forsaken the glory of God for some lesser glory. Set your sights on the glory of God, and your life will flood with joy like a dam set loose. There will not be a day that your life will not have meaning because you work for eternal glory. "You are not very impressive," some will imply. "I am not great, no." You may continue, "But my Master is great. My work may be small, but I work for the glory of His Kingdom — the greatest and the highest Kingdom. I delight to work for eternal riches and eternal glory. I am happiest in glorifying God... What is it you do again?"

# MORALITY

*There was a man in the land of Uz whose name was Job, and that man was blameless and upright, one who feared God and turned away from evil.*

**THE BOOK OF JOB**

*No books are so legible as the lives of men; no character so plain as their moral conduct.*

**JAMES H. AUGHEY**

*Morality may keep you out of jail, but it takes the blood of Jesus Christ to keep you out of hell.*

**CHARLES SPURGEON**

*You will never fade away, Your love is here to stay*
*By my side, in my life, shining through me everyday*
*You wake within me, wake within me*
*You're in my heart forever*

**HILLSONG YOUNG AND FREE**

*Keep them and do them, for that will be your wisdom and your understanding in the sight of the peoples, who, when they hear all these statutes, will say, 'Surely this great nation is a wise and understanding people.'*

**MOSES**

*It is shorter to state the things forbidden than the things permitted; precisely because most things are permitted and only a few things forbidden*

**G.K. CHESTERTON**

*And do not lead us into temptation, but deliver us from evil. For Yours is the kingdom and the power and the glory forever. Amen.*

**MATTHEW 6:13**

# MORALITY
## LOVE

## KINGDOMS

Different kingdoms have different rules for showing deference. In one kingdom, it may be proper to bow. In another, it may be proper to kneel. But, in every kingdom, it is good to honor the ruler either as an expression of gratitude or, perhaps, out of fear. In modern democracies, we are taught to express gratitude for our citizenship in the 'kingdom' by exercising our right to vote, seeking the welfare of our cities, and loving our neighbors. Despite our sin natures and broken kingdoms, this rule of 'love your neighbor' persists as an echo of a Kingdom which lasts forever and a King who is good. The only Good King has scripted eternity into lesser kingdoms that his children would believe and enter his greater Kingdom. But, he does not allow traitors who masquerade as his own enter his domain; he only lets his true citizens enter.

God, in his love and mercy, has adopted many of his former enemies into his Kingdom by making them sons. But, these children have not yet entered into his eternal Kingdom. We don't get transported to the heavenly realms the moment we receive citizenship through faith in Jesus. We wait in this lesser realm to tell of God's mercy and grace so that many sons may be brought to glory. While the children of God remain on earth, how are they to live? They do not need to work to enter the Kingdom for they have been granted full citizenship. How, then, does morality fit into the Christian life?

Men and women cannot go to heaven for being moral or decent or honorable — they must be perfect (John 3:3; Matt. 5:48; Col. 1:28). Morality is of no use to those who desire to enter the Kingdom of Heaven. The moral law, which all have broken, only condemns them as enemies of God. Any appeal to our own righteousness will be our condemnation. Humans break the moral law and cannot acquit themselves. In our own efforts, we would be guilty for all the ages of eternity. The eternal moral law, which supersedes time and space, stands ready to convict even the most 'moral' individual (Rom. 3:20; Luke 16:17; 21:33). Morality offers no forgiveness and no hope — only condemnation. Morality is a hellish master — unrelenting and unmerciful.

The moral law demands justice, and it is only proper for a criminal to be brought to justice. If someone steals from you, it is appropriate that they return the items they have stolen and serve the sentence demanded by the law. If someone spreads a lie about you, it is fitting that they apologize and tell the truth to all who heard the lie. Just payment is required for every evil.

The just penalty for breaking the law of God is death. Historically, the death penalty has been sentenced to murderers, not because their lives are not sacred, but because they have killed one who is sacred. Murder is an eternal matter; the life-flame of a precious immortal is extinguished. We, too, in breaking the eternal moral law of God, defile that which is precious. We desecrate a name that is eternally pure. Eternal punishment is only fitting.

But, haven't Christians been acquitted from the sentence of death? Don't they have a get-out-of-jail-free card? Here, we must make an important distinction. Christians are just as guilty as anyone else of breaking God's moral law. They are just as deserving of death because of their sin. Their sins must be punished, their sentence carried out. For the believer in Jesus, though, their death sentence has already been carried out — by Jesus himself.

By faith in the blood of Jesus, believers accept the atonement Jesus made for their sins. They are forgiven and made righteous, not by getting a free pass for their evil debts, but by receiving the full payment Jesus made to their account. As Paul says:

> I have been crucified with Christ. It is no longer I who live, but Christ who lives in me. And the life I now live in the flesh I live by faith in the Son of God, who loved me and gave himself for me. I do not nullify the grace of God, for if righteousness were through the law, then Christ died for no purpose. (Galatians 2:20-21)

The justice of God has been carried out upon sin forever in the eternal sacrifice of Jesus Christ. Because Jesus Christ is forever, the atonement is forever. Christians are no longer under the condemnation of the law. Christians have no obligation to the law because the law only applies to the sinful race of Adam. Jesus, who was born of the race of Adam, lived to put to death the law which Adam was under. He did so to create a new race — a race of eternally pure and glorious immortals raised to life by the power of God, commonly known as Christians (Rom. 8:29-30). Paul again makes this clear to the Christians in Rome:

Likewise, my brothers, you also have died to the law through the body of Christ, so that you may belong to another, to him who has been raised from the dead, in order that we may bear fruit for God. For while we were living in the flesh, our sinful passions, aroused by the law, were at work in our members to bear fruit for death. But now we are released from the law, having died to that which held us captive, so that we serve in the new way of the Spirit and not in the old way of the written code. (Romans 7:4-6)

Jesus Christ, with the Spirit of the power of his resurrection, has now brought everyone who has faith in Christ to new, eternal life (John 17:3). Christians now belong to the imperishable heavenly race of Jesus Christ. The law of Adam no longer convicts them because it has been abolished in their spiritual death. Christians live under a new law — the law of love — because they have been raised to new life. They have become new citizens of a new Kingdom, and the Kingdom has new rules. The new guiding principle? Love.

# LAW OF LOVE

It is often thought that the age of grace has no law. Hasn't the old law of morality, which only condemns people for sin, been torn up and thrown out? Yes, but when Jesus abolished the moral law by his death, he ushered in a new law. Grace freed us from the law of sin and death and granted us citizenship in the Kingdom of God where there is a law of love.

Immediately, when we learn that we are under the rule of law, even though it is one of love under the covenant of grace, we scoff at the idea. *I can do whatever I like. It matters not what I do — for I am under grace — and there is no condemnation for those under grace.* That is correct. There is no condemnation for those under grace. But, grace is far from the freedom to sin – that is bondage. Grace is freedom from the slavery of sin to live in love. Paul tells us that thinking we can continue living in sin because we are under grace is wrong thinking:

> What shall we say then? Are we to continue in sin that grace may abound? By no means! How can we who died to sin still live in it? Do you not know that all of us who have been baptized into Christ Jesus were baptized into his death? We were buried therefore with him by baptism into death, in order that, just as Christ was raised from the dead by the glory of the Father, we too might walk in newness of life. (Romans 6:1-4)

We have been made new. We now belong to a good and holy Master with a good and holy law.

It is only sin that makes us think 'law' is a bad word. The law is good. It protects citizens from the chaos of immorality (Rom. 13:3-4). It delivers justice to the oppressed and honor to all. It is only our criminal nature that desires to break the good and perfect law. Like a man who fears the government because he does not pay his taxes, we feared the law because we broke it. Good citizens who pay their taxes delight in the law, for they keep it and see roads, and bridges, and schools being built with the money. The one who keeps the law does not fear the law.

In the Old Testament, God gave the people of Israel the Greatest Commandment in what is known as the Shema (שְׁמַע). It begins: "Hear, O Israel! The LORD is our God, the LORD is one! You shall love the LORD your God with all your heart and with all your soul and with all your might" (Deut. 6:4-5; Lev. 19:18). This was the overarching rule for all of the Old Testament. Israel was to love God and love one another by keeping his commandments (Deut. 6).

Thus, the law was given to guide people in love for God and love for one another. It was meant to help humanity glorify God by keeping his commandments. But, since sin had ruined our ability to love God and others completely, the law was also given to suppress wickedness until the new law of the Spirit of love arrived (Gal. 3:24). God gave a good law to guide bad people until Christ came to give a new law and a new Spirit.

When Jesus came, he came to establish the New Constitution of a new Kingdom. All throughout the gospels (Matthew, Mark, Luke, John) Jesus is speaking of a New Commandment [Law] that we are to keep. It is remarkably similar to the old one:

> A new commandment I give to you, that you love one another: just as I have loved you, you also are to love one another (John 13:34).

> This is my commandment, that you love one another as I have loved you. (John 15:12)

> But I tell you, love your enemies and pray for those who persecute you, (Matthew 5:44)

> But when the Pharisees heard that he had silenced the Sadducees, they gathered together. And one of them, a lawyer, asked him [Jesus] a question to test him. "Teacher, which is the great commandment in the Law?" And he said to him, "You shall love the Lord your God with all your heart and with all your soul and with all your mind. This is the great and first commandment. And a second is like it: You shall love your neighbor as yourself. On these two commandments depend all the Law and the Prophets." (Matthew 22:34-40)

And one of the scribes came up and heard them disputing with one another, and seeing that he answered them well, asked him, "Which commandment is the most important of all?" Jesus answered, "The most important is, 'Hear, O Israel: The Lord our God, the Lord is one. And you shall love the Lord your God with all your heart and with all your soul and with all your mind and with all your strength.' The second is this: 'You shall love your neighbor as yourself.' There is no other commandment greater than these."
(Mark 12:28-31)

Jesus was teaching men and women that the New Covenant of the New Kingdom was about a New Law. But the new Law was very similar to the old: love God and love your neighbor. Jesus, in his brilliant wisdom, was summing up the entire Old Law in one new, complete and comprehensive law: love. As John points out, the new law of love that Christ taught was not new:

Beloved, I am not writing you a new commandment, but an old one, which you have had from the beginning. This commandment is the message you have heard. Then again, I am also writing you a new commandment, which is true in Him and also in you. For the darkness is fading and the true light is already shining. Whoever says he is in the light and hates his brother is still in darkness. Whoever loves his brother abides in the light, and in him there is no cause for stumbling. (1 John 2:7-10)

This is the message you have heard from the beginning: We should love one another.
(1 John 3:11)

And now I ask you, dear lady—not as though I were writing you a new commandment, but the one we have had from the beginning—that we love one another. (2 John 1:5)

So, if the law of love remains constant, how can we keep it any better under Christ? We can keep it because we no longer have to keep it in our own strength. God, in his mercy, promised to give us a new Spirit. God promised to give us his *own* Spirit to make us wholly righteous. He promised to give us a new *desire* and *power* to keep the Law of Love:

> And I will give them one heart, and put a new spirit within them. And I will take the heart of stone out of their flesh and give them a heart of flesh, that they may walk in My statutes and keep My ordinances and do them. Then they will be My people, and I shall be their God.
> (Ezekiel 11:19-20)

> And I will give you a new heart, and a new spirit I will put within you. And I will remove the heart of stone from your flesh and give you a heart of flesh. And I will put my Spirit within you, and cause you to walk in my statutes and be careful to obey my rules. (Ezekiel 36:26-27)

> For I will pour water on the thirsty land, and streams on the dry ground; I will pour my Spirit upon your offspring, and my blessing on your descendants. (Isaiah 44:3)

> I will give them a heart to know that I am the LORD, and they shall be my people and I will be their God, for they shall return to me with their whole heart. (Jeremiah 24:7)

> And I will ask the Father, and he will give you
> another Helper, to be with you forever, even the
> Spirit of truth, whom the world cannot receive,
> because it neither sees him nor knows him. You
> know him, for he dwells with you and will be in
> you. (John 14:16-17)

God has fulfilled his promises. All who have believed in
Jesus Christ have received the Holy Spirit of God (Acts 2:38-39;
Rom. 5:5). The Old Law has been abolished by the death of Jesus Christ, and all who believe in him have been raised to life as
children of the Living God. "For the law of the Spirit of life has
set you free in Christ Jesus from the law of sin and death" Paul
says in Romans 8:2. Men and women who have received the Holy
Spirit by faith now live in freedom under a new law of the Spirit
of life. The old has passed away and the new has come.

# LIFE OF LOVE

Now that we have been freed to live under the law of love,
we are to live a life of love. If true love for others starts with love
for God, how do we love God? Love for God is carried out differ-
ently than love for others. Love is an internal disposition of the
heart which desires another's good — their wellbeing and whole-
ness. Perhaps we want others to feel valued or cherished. Maybe
we give them a gift or meet their needs to show our love. But,
God is already complete; we cannot give to God anything physical or emotional to improve his wellbeing. He is whole in himself.

How, then, do we love God? We obey him. We prove our
love for him through our actions. Here, we see an example in human relationships. Consider a husband and wife. We would say
that a man who declares his love for his wife, yet withholds his
affection for her in word, thought, or action, is not actually loving

her well. If a man truly loves his wife, he will prove his love for her in his actions. So it is with God.

Throughout the New Testament, love for God is described as an internal disposition of the heart to honor God. "For I desire steadfast love and not sacrifice," God declares in Hosea 6:6, "the knowledge of God rather than burnt offerings." There is no greater honor given to a superior than to obey their command. Love for God is to honor his Name by keeping his word. Jesus himself reveals to us that if we love him, we will obey him:

> If you love Me, you will keep My commandments. (John 14:15)

> Whoever has My commandments and keeps them is the one who loves Me. The one who loves Me will be loved by My Father, and I will love him and reveal Myself to him." (John 14:21)

> Jesus replied, "If anyone loves Me, he will keep My word. My Father will love him, and we will come to him and make Our home with him. (John 14:23)

> If you keep My commandments, you will remain in My love, just as I have kept My Father's commandments and remain in His love. (John 15:10)

Love for God is obedience to God. Obedience is the mark of those who have been made righteous. Those who live in love are not trying to earn the grace of God. The grace of God, which has been given as a gift to those who believe, is the power by which Christians live a life of love.

Christians have received the love of God in abundance through the grace poured out through Jesus Christ. Christians are, therefore, rich in love. It is very easy to give what is not ours.

When money is given to us, it is much easier to give it away. It is easier still when it is given in unmeasurable abundance. So it is with Christians. Christians have received love by the grace of God through Jesus Christ in unending abundance. They now possess an endless spring of love overflowing in their souls like a cup set under a running faucet. Love for God proven by obedience to his commands is the natural response of love poured into the heart.

Love for God displayed in obedience is the mark of those who are the true children of God. It is the children of the home who know the rules of the house and keep them. Strangers do not know the rules and do not desire to keep the rules because they have no love for the master. Love for the Master — honor for his Name — is demonstrated by obeying his commandments and the mark of those who are true children of God:

> By this we can be sure that we have come to know Him: if we keep His commandments. (1 John 2:3)

> But if anyone keeps His word, the love of God has been truly perfected in him. By this we know that we are in Him: whoever says he abides in him ought to walk in the same way in which he walked. (1 John 2:5-6)

> By this we know that we love the children of God: when we love God and keep His commandments. For this is the love of God, that we keep His commandments. And His commandments are not burdensome. (1 John 5:2-3)

> And this is love, that we walk according to His commandments. This is the very commandment you have heard from the beginning, that you must walk in love. (2 John 1:6)

The children of God obey God. To disobey God is to worship some created thing more than God. It is idolatry (1 Sam. 15:23). Jesus has some harsh words for people who falsely believe that Jesus is their Lord yet do not do what he says. Habitual, unrepentant sin is a fruit of the tree of the unredeemed (Eph.5:5-6; Matt. 7:16-20). We cannot say that we love our parents or superiors and then disobey their word — that is the work of hate. Neither do we truly love God if we do not keep his commands. If we have been purchased by the grace of God, we will bear the fruit of righteousness. The Bible exclaims ardently that we are self-deceived if we believe that we love God and yet live in knowing disobedience:

> Not everyone who says to Me, "Lord, Lord," will enter the kingdom of heaven, but only he who does the will of My Father in heaven.
> (Matthew 7:21)

> Everyone then who hears these words of mine and does them will be like a wise man who built his house on the rock. And the rain fell, and the floods came, and the winds blew and beat on that house, but it did not fall, because it had been founded on the rock. And everyone who hears these words of mine and does not do them will be like a foolish man who built his house on the sand. And the rain fell, and the floods came, and the winds blew and beat against that house, and it fell, and great was the fall of it. (Matthew 7:24-27)

> The good man brings good things out of the good treasure of his heart, and the evil man brings evil things out of the evil treasure of his heart. For out of the overflow of the heart, the mouth speaks.

Why do you call Me "Lord, Lord," but not do what I say? (Luke 6:45-46)

For it is not the hearers of the Law who are righteous before God, but it is the doers of the Law who will be declared righteous. (Romans 2:13)

Be doers of the word, and not hearers only. Otherwise, you are deceiving yourselves. (James 1:22)

But the one who looks intently into the perfect law of freedom, and continues to do so — not being a forgetful hearer, but an effective doer — he will be blessed in what he does. (James 1:25)

What good is it, my brothers, if someone says he has faith but does not have works? Can that faith save him? (James 2:14)

If anyone says, "I know Him," but does not keep His commandments, he is a liar, and the truth is not in him. (1 John 2:4)

Everyone who makes a practice of sinning also practices lawlessness; sin is lawlessness. You know that he appeared in order to take away sins, and in him there is no sin. No one who abides in him keeps on sinning; no one who keeps on sinning has either seen him or known him. Little children, let no one deceive you. Whoever practices righteousness is righteous, as he is righteous. Whoever makes a practice of sinning is of the devil, for the devil has been sinning from the beginning. The reason the Son of God appeared was to destroy the works of the devil. No one born of God makes a practice of sinning, for

God's seed abides in him; and he cannot keep on sinning, because he has been born of God. By this it is evident who are the children of God, and who are the children of the devil: whoever does not practice righteousness is not of God, nor is the one who does not love his brother.
(1 John 3:4-10)

The fact that God expects us to obey his commands confuses some believers. Perhaps they look at those verses and believe they have to take their salvation back into their own hands, earning God's favor and forgiveness. They fall into legalism, adding rules to the gospel and working for their own righteousness. Others may read those verses and feel hopeless, seeing that they could never obey Jesus' commands fully and wondering if they could truly be saved.

Both parties would be missing the point. First, obeying God's commands is exactly the opposite of legalism — of needing to work to earn God's love. Obedience to the commands of God is a *response* to the love of God that we already possess in full measure. *Because* we have been granted God's favor, we are free from the oppressive rule of morality, which we could never perfectly keep despite our best efforts. *Because* we have already been forgiven, we are empowered to love God and others by the power of Holy Spirit within us. We acknowledge that any righteousness we possess was given by Christ (2 Cor.5:21), and that we have nothing to boast in but God.

Second, obeying God's commands produces joy rather than hopelessness. Rather than living in a constant state of unworthiness and guilt, we acknowledge that believers who remain on earth still battle a sin nature. Though we have been favored, forgiven, and adopted into the family of God, we still struggle with sin and do not yet love perfectly. We are being transformed like an adolescent child becoming an adult. It is a season of awkward growth. We may war between being a child and a grown up, but we live our lives full of hope because we believe that God will finish the good work he promises to complete in us.

Whether we battle self-righteousness or self-loathing, any hope of living a life of obedience rests fully on the power of God living inside of us. As we humbly seek to walk in the law of love, we war not to *become* children of God, for we have been made righteous in God's sight, clothed in Jesus' own righteousness. We battle, instead, to live in the victory that has already been won over the enemy of sin that once enslaved us. Our best defense is to ask God to remind us of that identity. We who were once under a brutal master have been purchased and adopted into a Royal Family:

> But you are a chosen race, a royal priesthood, a holy nation, a people for God's own possession, that you may proclaim the excellencies of him who has called you out of darkness into his marvelous light; for you once were not a people, but now you are the people of God; you had not received mercy, but now you have received mercy. (1 Peter 2:9-10)

Ultimately, those who are freed by God are free to love because they have *received* love. They have received the love of God through their great inheritance in Christ and through the gift of the Holy Spirit who dwells in them and satisfies them with steadfast love. It is this love that marks all of the genuine disciples of Christ:

> By this all men will know that you are My disciples, if you love one another. (John 13:35)

If anyone claims to be in the light but hates his brother, he is still in the darkness. (1 John 2:9)

But whoever hates his brother is in the darkness and walks in the darkness. He does not know where he is going, because the darkness has blinded his eyes. (1 John 2:11)

We know that we have passed from death to life, because we love our brothers. The one who does not love remains in death. Everyone who hates his brother is a murderer, and you know that no murderer has eternal life abiding in him.
(1 John 3:14)

If anyone with earthly possessions sees his brother in need, but withholds his compassion from him, how can the love of God abide in him?
(1 John 3:17)

Beloved, let us love one another, because love comes from God. Everyone who loves has been born of God and knows God. Anyone who does not love does not know God, because God is love.
(1 John 4:7-8)

We love because he first loved us. If anyone says, "I love God," and hates his brother, he is a liar; for he who does not love his brother whom he has seen cannot love God whom he has not seen. And this commandment we have from him: whoever loves God must also love his brother.
(1 John 4:19-21)

Those who are of God have God in them, and God is love. Believers are made of a new substance. New blood flows through their veins and brings life to their souls – they cannot help but love because they have been given a limitless supply. This is amazing grace! That God loves his children even in their imperfection. Sinners become saints, and saints live in love. It is one marvel that by the design and power of God a caterpillar becomes a butterfly and the winter becomes summer. It is another marvel that a child grows into an adult. However, it is of extreme wonder and glory that a human — trapped in sin and destined to die — can be made pure and granted immortality by the power of God. Love is the way of the Kingdom of God, and love is the mark of the citizens of the Kingdom. If you find a citizen of the Kingdom of God you will find one who lives love.

# DESTINY

*Peace I leave with you; My peace I give to you. I do not give to you as the world gives. Do not let your hearts be troubled; do not be afraid.*
**JESUS**

*Not everyone who has made peace with God has realized the peace of God.*
**VANCE HAVNER**

*By your power, we will go*
*By your spirit, we are bold*
*If we're gonna stand, we stand as giants*
*If we're gonna walk, we walk as lions*
**SKILLET**

*A perfect faith would lift us absolutely above fear.*
**GEORGE MACDONALD**

*Even though I walk through the valley of the shadow of death, I will fear no evil, for you are with me.*
**DAVID, KING OF ISRAEL**

*Have courage for the great sorrows of life and patience for the small ones; and when you have laboriously accomplished your daily task, go to sleep in peace. God is awake.*
**VICTOR HUGO**

*You're God of the hills and valleys,*
*And I am not alone!*
**TAUREN WELLS**

# DESTINY
## PEACE

## POWER

We delight in power. In it, we see glimpses of a universe outside of our control and the potential for finding safety in someone else's strength. Depending on our vantage point, power brings either a sense of peace or terror. Think about a summer thunderstorm. The silent summer sky is suddenly lit with streaking light. Loud claps of thunder roar like an untamed lion, rattling the windows. Rain falls like a thick curtain, drowning out all other sounds. The power of nature is set on display, and it is a delightful show to watch — from inside. Finding yourself outside in a thunderstorm, exposed and without shelter, is a very different experience. Outside, the rain drowns everything that is not shielded by a canopy. Outside, thunder shakes to the core, and the lightning resembles more of a lethal weapon than a light show. The same power is on display, but your experience of that force depends upon your vantage point.

Looking down on that same storm from the window of an airplane is a breathtaking picture show. If, however, the plane finds itself in the middle of the storm, it feels more like a war. It is one marvel to watch the powerful Niagara River cascade in deafening sound from a safe distance. It is another to be helplessly swept away in its power. The untamed power of nature somehow calms our hearts and brings a sense of peace when we can watch it from safety. But when we are caught up in its power without refuge it is terrifying. Power can bring peace, but only if it is on our side.

Children who see their first thunderstorm teach us something about the relationship between peace and power. They watch the sky in amazement and look around the room to assess the reaction of others. Everyone tells them to keep looking at the storm, but the longer they look, the more terrible it becomes in their eyes. The lighting flashes close, and the thunder rumbles with might. Soon the child stumbles back from the window in wide-eyed fear. Tears start flowing, and the child runs to the safe embrace of mom. Unknown power creates anxiety in the child, who runs to the power that they know is safe.

As we grow older, our desire for peace under the guard of power remains. Our nations build massive militaries and nuclear arsenals. We store up large amounts of money. We protect our homes with powerful security systems. We increase our power because we long to lay our heads down on our pillows in peace.

Our peace is directly proportional to our faith in power. If a people are certain their military is strong, they will not fear at night. If they know their military is weak compared to the strength of an enemy nation, they will not rest easy. Anxiety is the result of a conscious or unconscious apprehension that the power we trust in will not be 1. Powerful enough to win victory in our situation or 2. Present to fight for us. If we believe either, we will fear.

If we are to experience peace in this life, we must know a great power and trust that power to be present and to fight for us. A baby may cry when their parents leave the room because the greatest power they know is no longer present. In the same way, we will know peace not only when we know power, but also when we know that power is for us and ever present. We are at peace when the champion is on our team. It is when they are on the opposing side that we tremble.

# WEAK GODS

Who doesn't love an underdog? Think about how many great stories follow that plot line: *Of Mice and Men, The Lord of the Rings, Oliver Twist, Jane Eyre, Harry Potter, The Hunger Games, Holes, Life of Pi, The Count of Monte Cristo, Star Wars, The Hunchback of Notre Dame, Les Misérables, Forrest Gump, the Tortoise and the Hare...* The list is long. We never tire of seeing the one who was counted out crowned as a victor. The underdog trope resonates so well with the human conscious because, to some degree, we all feel that we are underdogs. We can relate to weakness.

Even more powerful than the underdog archetype in works of fiction are the true underdog stories. *Unbroken*, the incredible story of Louis Zamperini; *Miracle*, the unlikely story of the 1980 U.S. Men's Olympic Hockey team; *Braveheart*, the sobering story of William Wallace, a Scottish warrior who led his people to independence against King Edward I of England; *Apollo 13*, the miraculous story of the seventh manned mission in the Apollo space program. When we see underdogs win, it gives us joy. In our bones it makes us believe that we can win, too. The victory of underdogs gives us hope that we can beat the odds.

However, hope is easily dashed by reality. Often, our dreams don't come true. Our life doesn't play out the way we thought it would. As soon as we put the book down, fantasies fizzle. When the credits role, we shuffle out of the theatre and into the grey of reality. Our souls long to hope, but our experience teaches that hope hurts. It lifts the heart with false notions and unrealistic expectations. Our own hearts whisper in our ears that hope is lost on underdogs. So what are people supposed to hope in? What power is there to bring peace? What object should we rest our faith upon?

If we cannot find peace, we naturally look for escape. If war is unrelenting in a country, its greatest hope is to find peace. But, in the midst of struggle, many will flee the land in the hopes of finding peace elsewhere. Similarly, we long for peace in our souls but usually believe it is found somewhere else. We long for a greater power.

Retreat from reality's conflicts is found in both healthy and unhealthy ways. It is healthy for someone to withdraw from work and rest at home with her family. It is healthy for someone to go out with his friends. It is not healthy to drown stress with a bottle or to get lost in the brief ecstasy of drugs. These unhealthy outlets only create bigger problems.

The opioid crisis, the staggering rates of anxiety, depression, and suicide are all effects of deficient peace. Of course, there are sometimes clinical reasons for all of these struggles, and anyone wrestling with these issues should seek professional help immediately. But, our conversation deals with issues of the soul. Ailments that no medical treatment can cure and no microscope can discover. These are the realms of peace that medication cannot reach and the realms that need healing most. If our pride will take a seat and listen for a moment, we may be able to hear the cry of our souls. If treatment has not left your soul with peace that surpasses understanding then there is a greater treatment yet to try. There is a higher path to peace.

We have seen how peace is found in the confidence of power. Whether it is a person's power — like mom's arms in the middle of a thunderstorm, or an object's power — like our house's ability to withstand the winds of the storm, we feel at peace when we rest in power. If peace is eluding us, then, perhaps we have placed our confidence, or faith, in the wrong person or object.

People and objects are powerful to provide a certain level of peace. At their best, police and military are powerful to provide for our safety, but perhaps not for our acceptance and love. Loving parents may be able to provide acceptance, but perhaps not security. Guns are powerful objects for protection, but they cannot protect us from the deadly poison of slander. Jobs are powerful to provide financial stability, but jobs cannot protect from a crisis of identity and meaning. Nuclear weapons are powerful to defend from external attack, but they cannot protect from anarchy within a nation. There are many powers on earth, but not a single one offers ironclad protection. The longer we live, the more we realize how vulnerable we really are — and we don't like it. Whenever the power that we trust in lets us down, it makes us uneasy. Anxiety is forever knocking on our door, seeking to make its home in our hearts.

Living among other humans requires us to place our trust in people and things. You may consider yourself a skeptical person, and therefore, above getting hurt or let down. Perhaps you imagine that you do not need to trust in any power to find peace. But, in the course of one day, you may choose to trust dozens of times. We make choices about buying that PS4 from Craigslist, giving Facebook permission to use facial recognition software, being open with doctors, driving through an intersection, and sitting in an antique rocking chair. All require our conscious or subconscious trust. Ultimately, what we choose to trust has everything to do with our peace.

We all choose to trust some power because we know that we cannot defend ourselves from everything on our own. The amount of faith, or soul rest, that we have in the person or object we trust will depend on their amount of power. Thus, our peace is proportional to the *power of the object* of our faith, not the *power of our own* faith. If the New York Yankees put a toddler on the mound to close the game in the bottom of the ninth, Yankee fans are not going to have much faith that they will win. "Just have faith," someone will say. "I have the faith of a child." A fan might reply, "But not faith in a child." No matter how much faith a fan might have in the toddler, the little one lacks the strength to throw the ball to the plate. There will be no hope for victory — not because there is no faith. There will be no hope because there is no power.

Our souls long for great power because in great power there is great peace. Many spiritual beliefs have forms of godliness and some apparent power. Consider 'modern spirituality', which comprises mystical notions of the universe's power mixed with the power of positive self-talk. According to mystic spirituality, we need only to discover and center upon a power beyond or inside of ourselves in order to unleash the peace of the universe. Stress may be relieved by practicing yoga, or we may increase our self-esteem by positive self-talk.

While deep breathing and positivity can bring encouragement, they still lack the power that brings lasting peace. We may feel empowered by mystic notions of spirituality, but none of these powers can raise a man from the dead. None of these powers can assure human beings that they are loved and cherished. Great faith may be placed in yoga or self-talk, but because they lack ultimate power — sovereign, unmovable, unapologetic, God-power — they do not give ultimate peace.

Great faith in weak power is of no use. However, small faith in great power is the first step in the right direction to true peace. Sometimes, in order to realign our faith, we have to see a demonstration of power. It happens even to God's chosen people. In 871-852 BC, Israel had turned from worshipping The LORD to follow other gods. Israel's King Ahab worshipped Baal, an Ancient Middle Eastern god of rain and dew. A prophet of God named Elijah had prophesied a severe drought, and with no rain, a famine occurred in the land. Naturally, Ahab was not fond of Elijah. Ahab was furious because the drought foretold by Elijah demonstrated the weakness of his god. Baal, the presupposed god of rain and dew, couldn't make it rain.

In turn, the nation of Israel was starting to get frustrated with Ahab because their king couldn't provide food. All along, Elijah had told Ahab that rain would never again come down except by his word (1 Kings 17:1). Elijah was making Ahab look foolish before his kingdom, and if the people didn't get food soon a coup was very likely. The tension was at a breaking point.

Elijah then called for a showdown of powers. He requested all of Israel to come to Mount Carmel along with the 450 prophets of Baal and 400 prophets of Asherah, another Canaanite god. That's a matchup of 950 prophets to 1. Elijah set the rules of the face-off. There were two altars built, one by Elijah to The LORD, the other by the prophets of Baal. A bull was to be placed on both altars, and no fire was to be lit. Both Elijah and the opposing prophets were to call upon their respective deities, and the one who answered by fire would prove to be God. The prophets of Baal accepted the challenge willingly. Extra-biblical sources reveal that Baal was thought to be the god of fire and lighting in addition to rain and dew.

Two altars. Two teams. One underdog. All of Israel watching. That's good T.V. All morning, the prophets of Baal 'limped' around their altar, shedding their own blood and calling out to please Baal — to no avail. At evening, Elijah prepared his altar and bull. But, he did something the prophets of Baal did not do. He had a trench dug around his altar and had his altar drowned with water until the water filled the moat. Then, Elijah prayed before the bloodied and misguided prophets of Baal and the people of Israel saying:

> LORD, God of Abraham, Isaac, and Israel, let it be known this day that you are God in Israel, and that I am your servant, and that I have done all these things at your word. Answer me, O LORD, answer me, that this people may know that you, O LORD, are God, and that you have turned their hearts back. (1 Kings 18:36-37)

Power was put to the test, and God answered by fire. The fire that fell from heaven was so hot that it "consumed the burnt offering and the wood and the stones and the dust, and licked up the water that was in the trench" (1 Kings 18:38). If there was any question about who God was, the question was answered. A jaw dropping display of power proved who was worthy of faith. The response recorded in Scripture matches what we would expect from such a powerful and miraculous display: "When all the people saw it, they fell on their faces and said, 'The LORD, he is God. The LORD, he is God'" (1 Kings 18:39). No questions were necessary to verify what they had seen. All that Israel could do was worship the LORD of power. And, the LORD was not done. He gave a great rain over Israel and proved again his sovereign power over all of creation. God showed that his power is worthy of faith.

Faith is only as good as the object it rests in. Peace is only as strong as the power that defends it. Wisdom rests in this truth: our greatest peace is found by placing our trust in the greatest power. Here lies the root of much of the anxiety and fear that grips our hearts. We have faith but not in the power of God. We have traded, like so many nations and peoples before us, the power and peace of God for weak gods. Weak gods have some power but not the soul-rest that we long for. Weak gods give weak peace because they have weak power.

Faith in ourselves leaves us with a power that can succumb to the slightest ailment. Hope in money will leave us dashed when it grows wings and flies away. Trust in friends is a good trust, but experience has proven these waters uncertain. It is good to be wise and to have insurance, and healthy friendships, and take care of our bodies and have a savings account. What is not good is to place the peace of our souls on these sandcastles that may crumble with any rising tide. If today's god is weak, tomorrow's hope is weak. If today's God is strong, our hope for tomorrow is sure.

It is always the right time to switch out the weak for the Strong. The same Strong God who answered the prayer of Elijah has not changed. He has not grown a gray hair or left himself go. He is forever unchanging — faithful when we are faithless and powerful when we are powerless. He alone is the foundation of peace because he is the pinnacle of power. Even a small amount of faith in God provides infinitely more peace than faith in anything else. If you have no faith, ask God for faith. If you have anxiety, ask yourself if you have a weak god. If you want a Strong God, he IS — ever present and unchanging. He is not anxious about tomorrow; he will be a Strong God tomorrow just as he is today.

## STRONG GOD

It is the nature of God that makes him worthy of faith. He is holy. Set apart and far above everyone and everything. There is no one like the LORD. His omniscience, his omnipresence, his omnipotence, all display his holy supremacy. Jesus clues us in to the fact that the nature of God is the foundation of our peace:

> "Therefore I tell you, do not be anxious about your life, what you will eat or what you will drink, nor about your body, what you will put on. Is not life more than food, and the body more than clothing? Look at the birds of the air: they neither sow nor reap nor gather into barns, and yet your heavenly Father feeds them. Are you not of more value than they? And which of you by being anxious can add a single hour to his span of life? And why are you anxious about clothing? Consider the lilies of the field, how they grow: they neither toil nor spin, yet I tell you, even Solomon in all his glory was not arrayed like one of these. But if God so clothes the grass of the field, which today is alive and tomorrow is thrown into the oven, will he not much more clothe you, O you of little faith? Therefore do not be anxious, saying, 'What shall we eat?' or 'What shall we drink?' or 'What shall we wear?' For the Gentiles seek after all these things, and your heavenly Father knows that you need them all. But seek first the kingdom of God and his righteousness, and all these things will be added to you." (Matthew 6:25-24)

Jesus' logic is simple. If God provides for the needs of lesser creations, then God will provide for the citizens of his Kingdom. Jesus unveils that peace begins with faith that God will provide for every need because he is able and because he loves. Life lived fearlessly in light of that truth is the result of true biblical faith.

"I believe in God!" you say. "You believe that God is one; you do well. Even the demons believe — and shudder!" (James 2:19). Belief in God is very different than faith in God. Belief is the first step towards faith, but belief alone will not bring peace. Belief may acknowledge that God exists and even that He is powerful, but deistic belief does not see that God is always loving and ever present in the lives of those who trust in him. Mere belief in God will never produce peace in the deep caverns of the soul — only faith can. Belief can be an indifferent intellectual idea, faith is a personal embrace.

I may believe that a chair can support my weight, but until I sit on it, I will not have the rest the chair provides. Most people believe in chairs. The only ones who have faith in chairs are those who sit on them. My faith is completed in my resting on the chair. So it is with God. Our soul will not rest until we are resting on God. Biblical faith in God happens when we are looking to no other thing for our soul's rest. Here is true faith: resting entirely upon Christ. Just a brief glimpse of the authority of Jesus shows his supreme power and worthiness of our faith:

Then I saw heaven opened, and behold, a white horse! The one sitting on it is called Faithful and True, and in righteousness he judges and makes war. His eyes are like a flame of fire, and on his head are many diadems, and he has a name written that no one knows but himself. He is clothed in a robe dipped in blood, and the name by which he is called is The Word of God. And the armies of heaven, arrayed in fine linen, white and pure, were following him on white horses. From his mouth comes a sharp sword with which to strike down the nations, and he will rule them with a rod of iron. He will tread the winepress of the fury of the wrath of God the Almighty. On his robe and on his thigh he has a name written, King of kings and Lord of lords. (Revelation 19:11-16)

That God is powerful is beyond doubt. He spoke the world into existence by the power of his Word. He raises the dead, heals the sick, walks on water, knows the future, and gives orders to demons. God is very much in control. But, the solitary fact that God is powerful does not give us peace. Knowing that an enemy nation is powerful would bring us fear and not peace. Our peace stems from our knowledge that God is powerful *and* forever present and loving.

All throughout Scripture God is saying the same message: Fear Not. It is a message that never goes out of style because we never stop worrying. We are prone to fear because we are prone to forget that God is our present peace. When we forget that God is our peace we set our faith in other objects. We get anxious because we know every other object of faith has weakness. God is power and incapable of defeat. He only puts up W's. It is why he is constantly reminding His people that He is with them:

> When you go out to war against your enemies, and see horses and chariots and an army larger than your own, you shall not be afraid of them, for the LORD your God is with you, who brought you up out of the land of Egypt.
> (Deuteronomy 20:1)

> Be strong and courageous. Do not fear or be in dread of them, for it is the LORD your God who goes with you. He will not leave you or forsake you. (Deuteronomy 31:6)

Have I not commanded you? Be strong and courageous. Do not be terrified; do not be discouraged, for the Lord your God will be with you wherever you go. (Joshua 1:9)

Be strong and courageous, do not fear or be dismayed because of the king of Assyria nor because of all the horde that is with him; for the one with us is greater than the one with him.
(2 Chronicles 32:7)

Fear not, for I am with you; be not dismayed, for I am your God; I will strengthen you, I will help you, I will uphold you with my righteous right hand. (Isaiah 41:10)

The LORD your God is in your midst, a mighty one who will save; he will rejoice over you with gladness; he will quiet you by his love; he will exult over you with loud singing. (Zephaniah 3:17)

Peace I leave with you; my peace I give to you. I do not give to you as the world gives. Do not let your hearts be troubled; do not be afraid.
(John 14:27)

Keep your life free from love of money, and be content with what you have, for he has said, "I will never leave you nor forsake you."
(Hebrews 13:5)

It is the very presence of God that gives Christians great hope in the midst of struggle.

Imagine a weary person searching for a place to sit at a theme park. She can only find rest in a seat if there is a seat nearby. Although she believes in the power of a chair or bench to hold her up, only the presence of a chair or bench will provide any real rest. Peace is the direct result of the actual presence of God because the presence of God exists in both power and love. Like a loving father standing at the side of his child, God stands beside his children. When children learn to ride a bike without training wheels, loving parents or friends will hold the back of their seat as they pedal around the yard. The children will be at peace because they trust the *presence* of their parent beside the bike, the *power* of their parent to steady the bike, and the *love* of their parent to desire their well-being on the bike.

The presence of the unleaded glory of the Holy Spirit is the satisfaction that the soul longs to know. Anxiety flees from the power of the glory of God. "The LORD is my light and my salvation; whom shall I fear?" David asks. "The LORD is the stronghold of my life; of whom shall I be afraid?" (Ps. 27:1). God's love has been eternally poured out on us in the Holy Spirit. Moses prayed, "Satisfy us in the morning with your steadfast love, that we may rejoice and be glad all our days." (Ps. 90:14). God's power + God's love + God's presence = our peace.

On one occasion, Jesus had spoken some hard words that caused many of his nominal disciples to desert. Seeing that the people were leaving, Jesus turned and said to his twelve disciples, "Do you want to go away as well?" Simon Peter answered him, "Lord, to whom shall we go? You have the words of eternal life, and we have believed, and have come to know, that you are the Holy One of God." (John 6:67-69) Peter recognized that Jesus was God; he had seen his power and his love. He was not willing to give up the presence of Christ for some weak god. Peter was not willing to leave Jesus because he would not forfeit true peace.

Each morning, we must decide either to forfeit peace or live in peace. We begin wrestling with our insufficiencies at the break of day. Few wake up thinking 'you have what it takes,' or 'you are beautiful.' The normal greetings of the morning are

'You're not good enough,' or 'you're alone.' Our peace is pick-pocketed before our feet hit the floor. When we forget the reality of the gospel, we can spend our whole day fumbling for peace.

How would your life change if the truth of the gospel was to be always at the forefront of your mind? *You are not lovely,* as you look in the mirror. "No I am not lovely, but God, who is beauty, has delighted in me and called me his own and made me righteous. I have been made of the love of heaven and am loved eternally in Christ. God delights in me."

*You are alone,* as you look around your room. "I am not alone. I have set the LORD always before me; because he is at my right hand, I shall not be shaken."

*You are insufficient,* as you consider the day ahead. "Undoubtedly. I do not have what it takes, but my God does. His sacrifice is sufficient. His grace is sufficient. There is now no condemnation for me because I am in Christ. My God will supply all my needs."

*You are weak,* as you encounter challenges and conflicts. "I am weak, but my God who strengthens me stands here at my right hand. He is my refuge and my strength, a very present help in trouble. I will not fear though the earth gives way, though the mountains be moved into the heart of the sea. In my weakness, my God is strong. So I am very strong indeed for my God upholds me."

Peace floods the soul when the truth is spoken. The truth of the gospel brings hope and satisfaction to the table of each new day. Speaking the truth by taking your thoughts captive is very different than positive self-talk. One is rooted in fantasy, the other in reality. One is rooted in pride, the other in humility. When we try to conjure up peace through our own pride, we only pull the rug out from under our own feet.

*You are not lovely.* "Yes I am lovely; I don't need the validation of others to be happy; I love me." Just as soon as I seem to talk my way out of one anxiety, another emerges: *But, you say mean things and your last boyfriend dumped you and you lied about that thing last week and...* Not acknowledging our weaknesses only exaggerates them in our souls. Choosing pride brings not hope and satisfaction, but fear and self-delusion to the morning table. We will live in fear that someone will discover the truth of who we are. We will masquerade as the person we try to convince ourselves we are each morning, praying no one will take off our mask.

If pride is the highway to anxiety, humility is the express lane to peace. It frees the heart from notions that it has to be something more or something else. Humility acknowledges weakness and fault. It does not mask them, it unveils them and appeals to God who is Strength and Perfection. Humility completely disarms anxiety because it rests solely upon God. Be afraid? The God who spoke the world into being stands at my right hand. Try to be something else? God has made me his own and given me the righteousness of Christ. Obtain more? What more could I have than eternal riches and a Royal inheritance? I will not trade my Strong God for a weak one. My God will never change. His love for me will never fade.

Though Jesus has promised to give us peace in this life, peace is not the absence of conflict. If someone believes in Jesus they should expect struggle. But, peace is the result of the rock-solid reality that in the midst of the struggle of daily life, God is standing close. The soul-rest that the Christian has among every problem they face is that God is present.

Jesus told his disciples that the formula to peace is not self-esteem, financial security, or positive thinking. According to Jesus, the formula of peace begins and ends with faith in him. "I have said these things to you," he said to his disciples, "that in me you may have peace. In the world you will have tribulation. But take heart; I have overcome the world" (John 16:33). When

Jesus sent out his disciples, he sent them with a reminder that he would be with them. "And behold, I am with you always, to the end of the age" (Matt. 28:20). The beginning and end of peace is Jesus. He is the present power of love that has promised he will never leave or forsake any of his own.

Peace is grounded in confident faith in the person of Jesus Christ, and it is actualized through faithful prayer. In prayer, we acknowledge that God alone is sovereign over all things and appeal to the power and wisdom of God to intervene in reality. Prayer humbles us to acknowledge our insufficiencies and seek the power of God to win our battles. God promises to look on everyone who humbles themselves. God speaks through Isaiah saying, "But this is the one to whom I will look: he who is humble and contrite in spirit and trembles at my word" (Is. 66:2). Prayer is the catalyst of peace that the Bible encourages all believers to engage:

> Cast your burden on the LORD, and he will sustain you; he will never permit the righteous to be moved. (Psalm 55:22)

> Rejoice in the Lord always; again I will say, rejoice. Let your reasonableness be known to everyone. The Lord is at hand; do not be anxious about anything, but in everything by prayer and supplication with thanksgiving let your requests be made known to God. And the peace of God, which surpasses all understanding, will guard your hearts and your minds in Christ Jesus. (Philippians 4:4-7)

> Cast your cares on him because He cares for you. (1 Peter 5:7)

Peace has already been won. Jesus has overcome the world. He presently sits as the ruler over the cosmos. He is present today in the Spirit of power in everyone who believes in his name. Though it has been ultimately defeated, evil has not yet ceased on earth; but, it is still only permitted to do as Christ commands. Jesus is in control.

Christians face the trials of life with confidence, hope, and peace because of God's power, his presence, and his love for his people. Christians are not confident because they are better; they are confident because their God is Strong. Their peace is rooted in the greatest power. The Strong God who upholds the world and cares for sparrows cares for them; so, they are at peace. The love of God is present in the glory of the Holy Spirit which satisfies their souls; so, they are at peace. If you have no peace, perhaps it is time to trade in your weak gods for a Strong One.

# DESTINY 2.0

*The Kingdom of Heaven is like treasure hidden in a field,*
*which a man found and covered up. Then in his joy he goes*
*and sells all that he has and buys that field.*
**JESUS**

*When we've been there ten thousand years,*
*Bright shining as the sun,*
*We've no less days to sing God's praise*
*Than when we first begun.*
**JOHN NEWTON**

*Never tell a child "you have a soul." Teach him,*
*you are a soul; you have a body.*
**GEORGE MACDONALD**

*To go to heaven, fully to enjoy God, is infinitely better than the most*
*pleasant accommodations here.*
**JONATHAN EDWARDS**

*I am the Alpha and the Omega, the first and the last,*
*the beginning and the end.*
**JESUS**

*You must either give up your sins or give up all hope of heaven.*
**CHARLES SPURGEON**

*The doctrine of the Kingdom of Heaven, which was the main teaching of*
*Jesus, is certainly one of the most revolutionary doctrines that ever stirred*
*and changed human thought.*
**H.G. WELLS**

# DESTINY 2.0
## JOY

## NEW

The famous new car smell. The wonder of a newborn. Powering on a brand new smart phone. There is something special about 'Newness.' We like fresh paint and carpet and clothes when there are no stains, wrinkles, or sags. 'New!' is the word that grabs attention because newness is what the soul secretly longs for.

Advertisers know this, which is why they do not plaster 'OLD' all over billboards and packaging. 'Old' is the boring reality that we already know. Old jobs don't get our hearts pounding in anticipation the night before our first day. Children rarely ask for the oldest model on the market. We want the new job, toy, or phone because the new one is more glorious.

Even the 'old' things we like bring us joy because they are rare or new to us. We stare at the couple chugging down the street in their pristine Model T because no one else has one. If everyone had a Model T, they would not be fun to have. Antique stores and garage sales exist because one person's trash is another one's newfound treasure.

If we are honest with ourselves, the newness that we are longing for is one that does not rust or go out of style. If we could buy a car that would never lose its shine, or a phone that would never need an update, we would. In our current reality, new always turns to old, and glory inevitably fades. But, take heart, for one day glory will never fade. New will be a constant state of being, and 'old' will be a word long since forgotten.

All things will be made new, God promised (Is. 43:19; Rev. 21:5). This is the great hope of Christianity. Genuine believers have hoped in the ultimate glory of heaven throughout the history of Christian faith. Earth and all her glory are beautiful, but she is aging and wearing out. Like a family staying in a hotel while their home is being built, it will do for now, but not forever. Christians have been content to work for the glory of their Master in the old world, but they are really longing to be at home in the new one.

Heaven is going to be totally new. God is not fixing up this place. God is going to tear down the old world so he can make a brand new one — a *good* one (2 Peter 3:10).

In Revelation, John records a vision that God gave him of the new heaven and the new earth. If God's word did not prove to be true, we would be tempted to use 'unbelievable' to describe the consummation of heaven and earth:

> Then I saw a new heaven and a new earth, for the first heaven and the first earth had passed away, and the sea was no more. And I saw the

holy city, New Jerusalem, coming down out of
heaven from God, prepared as a bride adorned
for her husband. And I heard a loud voice from
the throne saying, "Behold, the dwelling place of
God is with man. He will dwell with them, and
they will be his people, and God himself will be
with them as their God. He will wipe away every
tear from their eyes, and death shall be no more,
neither shall there be mourning, nor crying, nor
pain anymore, for the former things have passed
away." (Revelation 21:1-4)

New everything — literally. Not one hint of anything old.
The universe will put on a different outfit (Is. 34:4; Rev. 6:14).
Physics will not be the same, and knowledge as we know it will
pass away (1 Cor. 13:8). The science of the human body will be
reinvented because citizens of the Kingdom of heaven will have
new immortal bodies. The foundation of energy which we now
know will be made new because God's glory will power the cosmos. John shows us that, as a result, the perfection of heaven will
be eternal:

> Then the angel showed me the river of the water
> of life, bright as crystal, flowing from the throne
> of God and of the Lamb through the middle of
> the street of the city; also, on either side of the
> river, the tree of life with its twelve kinds of fruit,
> yielding its fruit each month. The leaves of the
> tree were for the healing of the nations. No longer
> will there be anything accursed, but the throne
> of God and of the Lamb will be in it, and his ser-
> vants will worship him. They will see his face, and
> his name will be on their foreheads. And night
> will be no more. They will need no light of lamp

or sun, for the Lord God will be their light, and
they will reign forever and ever.
(Revelation 22:1-5)

It is hard to imagine a place without anything old or
worn, but that is only because we have never known a perfect
world. Heaven is newness that never gets old. Forever there is
glory. New life is the only kind of life because there is no death.
In heaven, there is good in every sense of the word — no bad.
Joy is actualized. Our greatest desires are fulfilled by the glory of
God's presence. Pleasure is the state of being, and joy is the way
of life.

An eternity in heaven is the glorious hope of every believer in Jesus. But, before everything is made new, God has to
settle some scores. He has to vanquish his enemies and crush
evil. God has offered redemption to anyone who repents and believes in Jesus Christ, granting them access to heaven through
his righteousness.

But, there are winners and losers. There are those who go
to heaven and those who do not.

# VICTORY

Heaven is a place of purity and peace. It is the dwelling
place of a Holy God and the eternal abode of his holy people. No
evil. No impurity. No mistake. Everything in Heaven will exist at
a glorious maximum. No foul person or thing is going to sneak
in. God will admit only those whose names are written on the
guest list:

And I saw no temple in the city, for its temple is
the Lord God the Almighty and the Lamb. And
the city has no need of sun or moon to shine on
it, for the glory of God gives it light, and its lamp

is the Lamb. By its light will the nations walk, and
the kings of the earth will bring their glory into it,
and its gates will never be shut by day — and there
will be no night there. They will bring into it the
glory and the honor of the nations. But nothing
unclean will ever enter it, nor anyone who does
what is detestable or false, but only those who are
written in the Lamb's book of life.
(Revelation 21:22-27)

Every name not written in Jesus' registry will be denied
access to paradise. God makes no exceptions and allows no ex-
cuses. He is now giving humanity time to repent and believe in
Jesus, but there will come a day when grace will no longer be
extended.

Evil will be ended — crushed like grain. Justice will be
delivered perfectly for everyone. No score will be left unsettled.
God is going to reign in love, but before he does, he is going to
overcome every last one of his enemies. Before Jesus ushers in a
new era of perfection, he is going to conquer the great antago-
nist of the age: Satan. Christ has already shown his power over
Satan when he overcame death. The second act will be final. John
records the vision God gave him of the apocalyptic encounter:

And when the thousand years are ended, Satan
will be released from his prison and will come
out to deceive the nations that are at the four cor-
ners of the earth, Gog and Magog, to gather them
for battle; their number is like the sand of the sea.
And they marched up over the broad plain of the
earth and surrounded the camp of the saints and
the beloved city, but fire came down from heaven
and consumed them, and the devil who had deceived them was thrown into the lake of fire and

sulfur where the beast and the false prophet were,
and they will be tormented day and night forever
and ever. (Revelation 20:7-10)

The devil (Satan) will one day be cast into Hell. The fate of
Satan and his demons is already set. Evil has an expiration date.

The fate of Satan doesn't bother anyone. It brings us joy
when fictitious villains are defeated. The demise of Satan, whether people believe him to be real or not, holds similar appeal. The
great enemy of humankind defeated and cast into hell — a fitting
end to the drama of the ages. What trips people up is not that
God will conquer Satan and the demons, but that God will conquer *every* enemy — including those who have broken his law.

The sobering reality of justice is that it is just. It does not
pick favorites or make exceptions. Justice is impartial and righteous. It always does what is right and good. It enforces the law
perfectly. No bribes. No blackmail. No loophole. God is just. He
must judge evil, and he will cast Satan and every unrighteous
soul into hell.

Death is not the end for anyone. It does not matter what
we believe about the afterlife — according to the Bible, everyone
is going to be raised from the dead. However, not everyone is
going to be raised to eternal life. In the book of Daniel, we learn
that "those who sleep in the dust of the earth shall awake, some
to everlasting life, and some to shame and everlasting contempt"
(Daniel 12:2). Jesus himself taught the same truth of the resurrection of all to his disciples saying, "an hour is coming when all
who are in the tombs will hear his [Jesus'] voice and come out,
those who have done good to the resurrection of life, and those
who have done evil to the resurrection of judgment" (John 5:28-
29). Everyone will not sleep the sleep of death forever. We will
all live forever somewhere, and that place is determined by our
relationship with Jesus Christ.

After death, there is not a period of remedial training where we sit in a remote corner of the cosmos and think about what we have done before we are allowed to enter heaven. There is not one mention in all of Scripture about the idea of purgatory.

Though perhaps an unpopular belief, all of Scripture and Jesus both declare that we live once, die once, and stand before God once (Heb. 9:27; 2 Cor. 5:10; 1 John 4:17).

Everyone will be judged according to their actions. Celebrities, Darwin, Walt Disney, you, and I — we all will give an account to our Maker. Everything we do is recorded by God and will be presented before him one day. Our eternal future will be determined by the record.

On that day, the experience of believers will be different than the experience of those who do not believe. Hell is no concern for believers, for their sins have been forgiven. Those who have placed their hope in Christ in life stand before God after death with the perfect righteousness of Christ credited to their account. God sees Christ's perfection and deems the believer worthy to enter heaven by grace. Condemnation is not a concern of a Christian. Thus, when Christians give an account, they will be judged for their actions *as children of God* at what is known as the Judgment Seat, or the Bema Seat, of Christ. Rewards will be gained or lost based on their works in Christ (1 Cor. 3:8, 13-15; 4:5).

The Judgment Seat is not the only judgment, however; there is another. It is called the Great White Throne Judgment. Here, everyone who has not believed in Jesus Christ in life will stand to give an account of their works. The event gets its name from John's image in the book of Revelation of Jesus sitting upon a great white throne:

> Then I saw a great white throne and him who was seated on it. From his presence earth and sky fled

away, and no place was found for them. And I saw the dead, great and small, standing before the throne, and books were opened. Then another book was opened, which is the book of life. And the dead were judged by what was written in the books, according to what they had done. And the sea gave up the dead who were in it, Death and Hades gave up the dead who were in them, and they were judged, each one of them, according to what they had done. Then Death and Hades were thrown into the lake of fire. This is the second death, the lake of fire. And if anyone's name was not found written in the book of life, he was thrown into the lake of fire. (Revelation 20:11-15)

Anyone who takes the time to read Scripture will find that Hell is a very real place — a place that actually exists. Jesus vehemently warned of Hell and encouraged men and women to receive forgiveness from sin in His name (Luke 16:19–31; Matt. 4:17, 5:30, 18:8). Hell is not a situation that we are going through right now. It is not a state of mind. We live on earth, not Hell. Hell is an eternal place of punishment originally prepared for the devil and his angels (Matt. 25:41). Earthly suffering may feel like 'Hell,' but it is nothing compared to the reality and eternity of Hell.

*I do not like to think about Hell.* Does anyone? It is a terrible thought. But, Jesus who came preaching grace and truth did not shy away from speaking of Hell's reality. The prophets who came before him did not either (Ps. 9:17; Jude 7, 13; Ez. 18:20; Is. 66:22-24). It is the mercy of God that warned humanity of the penalty of unbelief and the eternal ache of hell. The Bible describes it as undying worm and unquenchable fire (Is.66:22-24; Mark 9:42-48), everlasting contempt (Dan. 12:2), eternal fire

(Luke 16:24; Matt. 18:8, 25:41), everlasting destruction (2 Thessalonians 1:5-10), gloom of utter darkness (Jude 13), torment of fire and sulfur (Rev. 14:9-11), and a Lake of Fire (Rev. 20:10, 14-15). Hell is an unending fate — a fever that never breaks. It was because men and women were destined for hell that Jesus came to save sinners from its horrors. It was his love that led him to speak of its terrors that we might repent.

True understanding of our salvation only comes with true understanding of Hell. Often we hear people saying that they were saved from themselves or from a situation or a person. And this is true, God is a God who daily bears us up. He is a present salvation, mighty to save, every day in the life of a believer (Ps. 68:19; Is. 41:10; 46:4). But, the ultimate deliverance of Jesus' salvation is from the wrath of God – a just fury poured out upon evil.

*Aha, see, I knew God was a bitter, angry God, I will never bow to such a one!* But, have we never been angry at those who have wronged us? Is it wrong to be angry or desire justice from those who have stolen from us? Of course not — it is only proper. The civil law exists to bring wrongdoers to justice. We would not call the civil law or the District Attorney bitter because they convict murderers, rapists, and thieves. The wrath of the civil law is designed to execute justice; it is not designed to be an act of hate. If a woman was attacked by a man or a small child wronged by a predator, is it not a most appropriate matter to bring the perpetrator to justice? We would think it cruel not to. The wrath of the civil law is not only appropriate, it is necessary.

In the same way, it is not mean of God to pour out his wrath. The eternal law of God and the eternal glory of God must be vindicated. God's wrath is just and necessary. It is just because the eternal punishment fits the eternal crime. It is necessary because the law, which reveals the depths of our sin natures, must be upheld. Any earthly notions of justice we possess have been taught to us by the justice of God. The just and necessary wrath of the civil law toward lawbreakers is only an image of the just and necessary wrath of God toward evil.

The wrath of the law is only terrifying to those who are under its penalty. No good citizen sits around and trembles at the thought of the death penalty — though it is a terrible and real terror. It is those who sit on death row who tremble at the sentence of death because they are destined for its wrath. In the same way, the wrath of God is not terrifying to those who are not destined to experience it. Those who believe in Christ do not sit and ponder the wrath of God. They speak of his grace, his love, and his mercy because they are citizens of his Kingdom and heirs of his glory. They once feared the wrath of God when they were children of wrath. Now they have received mercy by trusting in the death of Christ who absorbed the wrath of God on their behalf (Rom. 3:24-26). Only those who have not believed in Christ and received forgiveness for sins should fear the wrath of God, for they remain under it. "Whoever believes in the Son has eternal life," Jesus said, "whoever does not obey the Son shall not see life, but the wrath of God remains on him" (John 3:36). Awaiting wrath is a most dreadful thought, which is why many do not like to think of God or the afterlife. Our conscience whispers that we are guilty, and we feel dread.

Thus, there are only two perspectives through which to view the wrath of God. Either we see the just wrath of God as appeased by Christ on our behalf, or we see the wrath of God as our own bitter cup to drink. The wrath of God, then, is viewed either as a just act of the glory of God or as a mean and dreadful thing. It is as David said, "with the purified you show yourself pure; and with the crooked you make yourself seem tortuous" (Ps. 18:26). Like a criminal who despises the law because he fears its penalty, the unappeased wrath of God is a terror to entertain.

That God will defeat all of his enemies is beyond doubt. That he will pour out his just wrath upon evil is certain. God's word has revealed that absolute victory will be realized in time. Satan and all evil will be cast into eternal judgment. The time remains for anyone who calls upon the name of The LORD to be saved from the wrath of God. God has been victorious in conquering sin and death, just as he will be victorious in eternally conquering his enemies. The difference is, now he extends them his mercy, but there will come a day when he will extend his enemies no terms of peace. For those of us who are already in Christ, conversations of hell serve as reminders of the immeasurable mercies of God poured out on us and our calling to share the hope that we have found so that others might also experience joyful eternity with God.

# JOY

Everything will be new in Heaven Including people. Jesus was not just showing off when he died and rose from the dead. He was literally making it possible for eternal life to be given to mortal humans. He was actually stripping death of its power and making immortality a present reality. The victory of Jesus Christ over death changed everything. Just like a tree whose roots have been cut may bear green leaves for a time, death still persists on earth. Humans perish, and nature wears out and dries up. But, a tree without roots cannot live on forever, and the very roots of death were severed by Christ at the resurrection.

Christianity begins and ends with faith in the person of Jesus Christ. If Jesus Christ was not physically raised to life then the hope of Christianity is dead (1 Cor. 15:12-19). What good is salvation from sin if death is a dark unconscious end? Salvation with no resurrection is no good. Thankfully, Christ has been raised from the dead, and he appeared to many witnesses (Acts

1:3; 1 Cor. 15:3-11). His resurrection is manifested even today in the spiritual transformation of people who receive the Holy Spirit. Death is dead. Jesus is alive. Hope is certain.

The Apostle Paul was adamant that Christians understand the victory that Christ has won over death through his resurrection. The unshakeable hope of Christianity is that death is not the end. Real hope was born the day the God-man Jesus Christ rose from the dead so that we might be made alive forever. Paul comforts the doubters when he states:

> But in fact Christ has been raised from the dead, the firstfruits of those who have fallen asleep. For as by a man came death, by a man has come also the resurrection of the dead. For as in Adam all die, so also in Christ shall all be made alive. But each in his own order: Christ the firstfruits, then at his coming those who belong to Christ. Then comes the end, when he delivers the kingdom to God the Father after destroying every rule and every authority and power. For he must reign until he has put all his enemies under his feet. The last enemy to be destroyed is death. For "God has put all things in subjection under his feet." But when it says, "all things are put in subjection," it is plain that he is excepted who put all things in subjection under him. When all things are subjected to him, then the Son himself will also be subjected to him who put all things in subjection under him, that God may be all in all.
> (1 Corinthians 15:20-28)

Christ has literally put all things under his power — including death. When a Christian dies, the Bible is explicitly clear that they are immediately present with the LORD in a spiritual body (Luke 23:43; Phil. 1:23; 2 Cor. 5:8). Our physical bodies are still dead. The great hope that Christ brings is not only that believers are present with Christ immediately after death, but also that their bodies will one day be resurrected in immortal glory.

The real physical resurrection of Jesus Christ affords believers in Jesus the hope of a real physical resurrection of their own physical body. The same power of God that raised Christ from the dead will raise to life all who have trusted in him. The Christian hope of eternal life is not rooted in a distant mystical deism. It is rooted in the reality of the resurrection power of Jesus Christ (John 5:25-29). Paul explains to the Thessalonians:

> But we do not want you to be uninformed, brothers, about those who are asleep, that you may not grieve as others do who have no hope. For since we believe that Jesus died and rose again, even so, through Jesus, God will bring with him those who have fallen asleep. For this we declare to you by a word from the Lord, that we who are alive, who are left until the coming of the Lord, will not precede those who have fallen asleep. For the Lord himself will descend from heaven with a cry of command, with the voice of an archangel, and with the sound of the trumpet of God. And the dead in Christ will rise first. Then we who are alive, who are left, will be caught up together with them in the clouds to meet the Lord in the air, and so we will always be with the Lord. Therefore encourage one another with these words.
> (1 Thessalonians 4:13-18)

Everyone will be resurrected. Everyone will be made immortal. Whatever heavenly atoms comprise the risen body of Jesus Christ will be the atoms that form the bodies of the new immortal humanity. Though sin pulls humanity back to dust in death, dust cannot hold our flesh for eternity. Christ has conquered sin and death, and we will be raised with the imperishable atoms of Christ – never to die.

Immortality is the great hope of Heaven and the great horror of Hell. We have seen that Hell is a place of conscious torment. The same immortality that is a blessing in Heaven is a curse in Hell. Its inhabitants long to die, but death is impossible, for it is conquered. The body and soul are eroded forever in agony. On earth, one who falls in a deep pit has some hope for escape — if only by death. Hell offers no hope for escape. Immortality will keep him there forever in the deepest pits of agony and loneliness. The immortality longed for in life will be despised forever in Hell. I pray that everyone repents and never knows Hell.

To those who place their faith in Jesus' finished work of salvation, immortality will be a great joy of Heaven. Those who persevere to the end will be crowned as victors. Observing competitors cross the finish line in victory makes our own hearts rejoice. It is a primeval longing in our soul — the longing to win. Competitors cannot win a race, however, if they stop midway. If they stop running, they will be disqualified. The competitor who strives to the end in sweat and tears has great joy in raising their hands in victory. They fought the good fight, they finished the race, and they have kept the faith (2 Tim. 4:7-8).

Like a competitor, we cannot expect to enter Heaven without persevering through to the end. Jesus said, "The one who endures to the end will be saved" (Matt. 24:13). God is looking to crown winners who cross the finish line (2 Tim. 2:12; Heb. 10:36; 12:1-2; Rev. 3:11). Jesus spoke through John about the great reward that is given to everyone who perseveres:

And he who was seated on the throne said, "Behold, I am making all things new." Also he said, "Write this down, for these words are trustworthy and true." And he said to me, "It is done! I am the Alpha and the Omega, the beginning and the end. To the thirsty I will give from the spring of the water of life without payment. The one who conquers will have this heritage, and I will be his God and he will be my son. But as for the cowardly, the faithless, the detestable, as for murderers, the sexually immoral, sorcerers, idolaters, and all liars, their portion will be in the lake that burns with fire and sulfur, which is the second death." (Revelation 21:5-8)

If we're not careful, those verses can stir up fear in our hearts. *What if I'm not good enough to persevere? Sometimes I am cowardly and faithless...does this mean I can lose my salvation? How can I know that I am enduring in the race?*

When fear of our own unworthiness creeps into our hearts, we must remind ourselves of the amazing grace of the gospel. Our unworthiness is precisely why Jesus — God in flesh — came to earth. He understood our inability to persevere, so he persevered perfectly on our behalf. He ran the perfect race. He lived a completely righteous life so that, when we place our faith in *him*, he might credit his perfect perseverance to our account. Look at those verses again: *the one who conquers* will have this heritage. Jesus Christ is the one who persevered in life and conquered sin in his death and resurrection. We now have a High Priest who pleads our cause before the Judge. He IS the one who conquers, and when we rest in his finished work, we have a secure hope — a heritage with Christ.

Another promise of our secure salvation is the Holy Spirit who lives in us. He is given to us as a guarantee that we have been redeemed. He convicts us when we sin and helps us pursue lives that bring God glory. He ministers grace to our souls and shapes our hearts to look more like Jesus. When we walk in step with the Spirit, our lives bring forth good fruit: love, joy, patience, kindness, goodness, faithfulness, gentleness, self control (Gal. 5:22-23). We've seen how far own efforts take us — it is the work of the Holy Spirit that sanctifies us until we are crowned the victor's crown.

# THE FEAST

Marriages, funerals, and celebrations of victories mark the beginning of a new way of life or a new era of joy. After winners are crowned and enemies have been defeated, it is most appropriate to feast. The union of marriage is celebrated by a feast. Christian funerals are even concluded with a celebratory feast. Far from celebrating death, the attendants are celebrating a reunion, a homecoming.

One day, believers will take part in the great Marriage Supper of the Lamb to celebrate the reign of God and his Kingdom. In Revelation, John records his vision of the event:

Then I heard what seemed to be the voice of a great multitude, like the roar of many waters and like the sound of mighty peals of thunder, crying out,

"Hallelujah!
For the Lord our God
The Almighty reigns.
Let us rejoice and exult
And give him the glory,

For the marriage of the Lamb has come,
And his Bride has made herself ready;
It was granted her to clothe herself
With fine linen, bright and pure"—
For the fine linen is the righteous deeds of the
saints.

And the angel said to me, "Write this: Blessed are
those who are invited to the marriage supper of
the Lamb." And he said to me, "These are the true
words of God." (Revelation 19:6-9)

"Joy is the serious business of heaven," wrote C.S. Lewis. What it will be truly like, heaven only knows. Evil will be no more. Death and disease will be finished. 'Hope' will be an unnecessary word, for hope will be fulfilled in perfect glory. Tears will be wiped away. Tragedy will be reserved for a genre of theatre. Love will rule in merciful tyranny. Lions will lay down with lambs. Light will be pure, and forever will be tomorrow. God will be with his people, and his people will be with their God.

Heaven is the fulfillment of every notion of beauty and pleasure that ever etched itself on the soul. If today is long and miserable, let not your heart be troubled. Eternity with God is long and joyful. Long has the soul waited for Heaven, and long shall it be satisfied. Long have God's people cried out for his salvation, and long they shall receive it.

Once, in the town of Earth, odd little children walked about in unflattering garments. Some townspeople shook their heads, others looked at the children in disgust. Some overtly mocked them for their rags, and others quietly asked the children to trade them for more desirable clothes. The children smiled and declined, happily wearing their tattered robes. They lived with joy despite the actions and reactions of the people of Earth, for they possessed hope. See, the townspeople didn't know that the children had been promised a gift beyond what they or anyone else could imagine. One day, as the townspeople mocked their clothes, the children not only received royal robes, but also a crown, for they had inherited the world.

# NOTES

## TRUTH: RIGHT IN FRONT OF US

1. Emphasis added.
2. C.S. Lewis, "Mere Christianity," in *The Complete C.S. Lewis Signature Classis* (New York, NY: Harper One, 2002), 12.
3. J. Maxwell Miller, and John H. Hayes, *A History of Ancient Israel and Judah* (Louisville, KY: Westminster John Knox Press, 1986) 60.
4. Eugene Carpenter, "Archaeology and the Old Testament," in *Christian Apologetics: An Anthology of Primary Sources*, ed. Khaldoun A. Sweiss and Chad V. Meister (Grand Rapids, MI: Zondervan, 2012), 295-307. See also: Dr. Stephen Meyer, *True U: Is the Bible Reliable?* DVD (Colorado Springs, CO: Focus on the Family), 2011.
5. Gary R. Habermas, "Experiences of the Risen Jesus," in *Christian Apologetics: An Anthology of Primary Sources*, ed. Khaldoun A. Sweiss and Chad V. Meister (Grand Rapids, MI: Zondervan, 2012), 354-361. See also: *Douglas Groothuis, Christian Apologetics: A Com-*

*prehensive Case for Biblical Faith* (Downers Grove: InterVarsity Press, 2011), 527-563.

# ORIGIN: THE POWER OF THE WORD

1. Robin Collins, "A Recent Fin-Tuning Design Argument," in *Christian Apologetics: An Anthology of Primary Sources*, ed. Khaldoun A. Sweiss and Chad V. Meister (Grand Rapids, MI: Zondervan, 2012), 107. See also: drcraigvideos, "The Fine-Tuning of the Universe," Filmed [June 2016]. YouTube video, 06:22. Posted [June 2016]. https://www.youtube.com/watch?v=EE76nwimuT0.

# ORIGIN 2.0: HOW DID WE GET HERE?

1. That amazing number includes Enoch, who really threw off the average when he was taken up into heaven by God at the tender age of 365. Without including Enoch, the average age rises to 912.2 years).

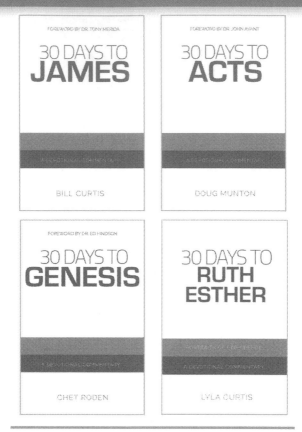

*Also from Seed Publishing:*

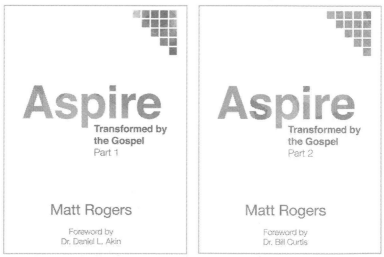

.